ALL ALONG THE
WATCHTOWER

MURDER AT FORT DEVINS

WILLIAM CRAIG

WILD BLUE
PRESS

WildBluePress.com

ALL ALONG THE WATCHTOWER published by:
WILDBLUE PRESS
P.O. Box 102440
Denver, Colorado 80250

Copyright 2022 by William J. Craig

WILDBLUE PRESS is registered at the U.S. Patent and Trademark Offices.

ISBN 978-1-957288-26-0 Hardcover
ISBN 978-1-957288-25-3 Trade Paperback
ISBN 978-1-957288-24-6 eBook

Cover design © 2022 WildBlue Press. All rights reserved.

Interior Formatting/Cover Design by Elijah Toten
www.totencreative.com

ALL ALONG THE WATCHTOWER

Table of Contents

PROLOGUE

A red Ford 4x4 F150 pickup truck pulls to a stop on Washington Street in Ayer, Massachusetts with its left blinker on, awaiting the oncoming traffic. Once the last car passes, the truck pulls into an apartment complex parking lot. In the truck is Green Beret William Tyree and his wife, Elaine. They pull into a parking spot and Elaine gets out of the vehicle. She walks over to the driver's side of the truck, gives her husband a kiss, and proceeds to head up the front stairs to her apartment building. She waves to him as she heads into the building and he waves back as he begins to pull back out onto Washington Street.

Suddenly, the silence of the afternoon is broken when Elaine's voice is heard screaming, "Get out of here! Leave me alone!" The neighbor in the next apartment phones the police and attempts to get a response from the apartment but to no avail.

Once the landlord is reached, he goes to the building to open the apartment for the police. There are traces of blood splatter on the door and in the hallway outside the apartment. When the door is opened, no one expects to see Elaine Tyree lying face up in her army fatigues. The apartment shows signs of a struggle. Clean laundry is strewn about and a lamp has been knocked over. The scene provokes skepticism in the investigators. Did Elaine Tyree walk in on an attempted robbery or was someone she knew behind her murder?

Everyone present that day at 104 ½ Washington Street, Apartment 1 soon finds themselves plunged into an eerie netherworld of secrets and lies, as new and mystifying leads suggest that the crime could have been perpetrated by the US government.

Not only does this murder shake a sleepy New England town to its core, but it also has far-reaching implications concerning the United States Army, the Ayer Police Department, the US Army Criminal Investigation Division, and the Massachusetts judicial system.

"How lucky I am to have something that makes saying goodbye so hard." A.A. Milne

CHAPTER ONE

The Unreal Dream

William Tyree grew up believing that the United States Army was the greatest institution in the world. He saw himself as the next great defender in a long line of military men. The Tyree men had served in the US Army since 1847, so it didn't come as a surprise when he dropped out of high school to join the military.

William "Bill" Tyree stands at five foot, eleven inches with short blond hair, hazel eyes, and a swimmer's build, weighing in at 142 pounds. Bill was born at Fort Sill, Oklahoma to United States Army First Sergeant William Murray Tyree Sr. and Gaye Tyree. He is the middle child of five, three boys and two girls. His father was a career army noncommissioned officer who retired and settled in Kearns, Utah in February 1968. For all intents and purposes, Tyree grew up as an army brat and traveled around the world wherever his father was stationed. Shortly thereafter, the family again moved to Riverton, Utah, where his parents purchased a home. He attended West Jordan Jr. High School, which he completed. He then attended Bingham High School in Copperton, Utah.

Bill Tyree decided that his future would be better served in the United States Army rather than staying and completing high school. After getting a GED, Bill hitchhiked twenty-seven miles to the army recruiting station in Granger, Utah.

While talking with the recruiter, he requested to be assigned to the 82nd Airborne Division. He made this request because the Special Forces weren't taking any new recruits in March 1975. Bill had done his research concerning his options for career fields. He wanted a career field that ensured he would have the best training and the most excitement. This is why he requested an assignment to the 82nd Airborne Division. He also knew that the Green Berets would draw men from the 82nd Airborne Division whenever they needed to replenish their ranks before they would take an enlistee straight out of basic training. He was hoping to be one of these men.

Bill recalls his first couple months at Fort Bragg ."While at Fort Bragg, I became involved with a variety of military schools, and eventually became associated with a number of Green Berets who were assigned to the US Army Special Forces, also stationed at Fort Bragg. I studied small arms and foreign languages while associating with Special Forces soldiers, and also took courses from a civilian college in Fayetteville, North Carolina, which is located adjacent to Fort Bragg."

In November 1976, Bill was discharged from his first enlistment. The discharge is related to a parachuting accident in October 1976. He received an honorable discharge due to a family hardship. This discharge allowed him to return to active duty when he was in better health. As he packed his bags and said his goodbyes before leaving Fort Bragg, his buddy reminded him that he had only been on post for three months of his entire enlistment and that his brother had let it slip that he had seen Bill in Panama. His friend also attempted to have him elaborate further about the injury and scar on the right side of his nose, but Tyree artfully dodged the questions. He denied the allegations and shook hands with his pal before heading out of the barracks and back to civilian life. It is not uncommon for soldiers to have signed a military Classified Non-Disclosure Agreement, otherwise known as a form SF-312. This practice is to ensure that classified information stays that way.

When Bill got back home to Utah, he found work washing cars at Butterfield Ford. While home, he bumped into his first love, Denise, whom he knew from grade school. The two of them had an instant connection and began dating. While he was at home in June 1977, Bill met Ken Garcy, a soldier in camouflage fatigues with a green beret in his pocket. He was beating the hell out of four of the local tough guys outside George's Bar in Riverton, Utah. Garcy and Bill began a conversation when he noticed Bill watching the fight from his motorcycle. Bill informed Garcy that he was prior service and had the same training that Garcy demonstrated in the fight. Almost instantly, they became friends. Garcy was with the 10th Special Forces Group Airborne training at Camp Williams. This post was down the road from Bill's parents' home. A few days later, Bill ran into Garcy again, along with SFC Mike Menzie, Captain Jack Brewer, and Major Watty Smith outside a laundromat in Riverton, Utah. Bill and the men began discussing his former MOSs (Military Occupational Skills). The men quickly took to Bill and they asked him if he was going back to the military. Bill replied that he was unsure and Mike Menzie informed him that if he decided to reenlist to look him up when he got to the 10th Special Forces Group at Fort Devens.

Bill left Butterfield Ford and began working at a civil service position that became available at the Tooele Army Depot. The depot stored, issued, received, renovated, modified, maintained, and demilitarized conventional munitions. At this job, he would be able to utilize his army training in chemical/biological/nuclear warfare. He earned more money than he had at his other job. His job at the depot was to go to the concrete bunkers and count the chemical and biological weapons, and act as security during transshipments.

As Bill considered going back into the military, his relationship with Denise began to deteriorate. She informed her mother and a bishop at the Mormon Church of every aspect of her relationship with Bill. This became a distressing issue between the two of them, and he and Denise mutually decided to call it quits due to her convictions about not leaving the Mormon Church.

In July 1977, Bill passed through the doors of yet another US Army recruiter. Here he talked with a staff sergeant who was on temporary duty from the 10th SFG (A). Tyree requested duty and training with the 10th SFG (A) and they began the entrance paperwork for prior service.

On August 21, 1977, William Tyree reported for duty at Bravo Company 1st Battalion, Fort Lee, Virginia. Bravo Company was one of two co-ed training companies. He checked in with long hair, lamb chop sideburns, tinted aviator glasses, and dressed in civilian clothes. Bill was standing off in the distance watching First Sgt. Aponte chew out Bravo Company over various barracks infractions. When Aponte was finally done, he approached Bill.

Aponte asked, "When did you report in?"

Bill replied, "I reported last night to the charge of quarters and was told to be at the orderly room at 0900 hours."

Aponte said, "Get into a duty uniform, shave, and get a haircut. Then report to the orderly room at 1300 hours."

Bill followed the orders to the letter. He reported wearing permanent press fatigues with school badges, Airborne wings, aviator crewman's wings, and a Pathfinder badge. It was highly unusual for an Airborne qualified soldier to be assigned to the unit.

In August 1977, Bill attended a party at the Holiday Inn at St. Petersburg, Virginia. He met a young woman in passing named Elaine Hebb, who was also stationed at Fort Lee, while he was in between jumping off the third-floor balcony railing with other men into the hotel pool. This chance encounter with a pretty girl would have everlasting consequences for Bill and his future. The next time he would see Elaine was on Labor Day weekend of 1977. Bill was eating in Charlie Company's mess hall when he got up to get a glass of milk. Elaine took his seat and the two of them were inseparable for the rest of the day.

Elaine and Bill began dating and within a short time they became serious. Bill recalls, "She had taken my chair by mistake and a genuine spark was shared. After that when we were not on duty, we hung around together. We discussed getting married as soon as we met. It just seemed like the right thing to do."

Elaine was a couple years older than Bill. She was a pleasant girl who had not really dated or been exposed to the outside world while growing up in Maryland. She was a very private person who didn't socialize like other girls her age.

Elaine's best friend while in the army was Tina Gregory. The two of them had met at Fort McClellan in Alabama. Later, the two women were transferred to Fort Lee, Virginia and were roommates. While at Fort Lee, Elaine was questioned by the Army Criminal Investigation Division, otherwise known as the CID. They wanted to know if she had any information about a loan sharking operation that was operating on post. According to Tina Gregory, she too had been questioned and they both denied any knowledge of the activities in question. However, their denial couldn't be further from the truth.

Elaine was an avid writer who kept two diaries. The first contained her personal thoughts. The second diary, however, was different. It contained any and all information and gossip she overheard or witnessed on post. Much of the information centered on illegal activities. In this second diary was the information that the CID was looking for. It was widely believed that a soldier named Tim Cummings was involved with loan sharking. If he was, Elaine would never tell. Tina believed Elaine wrote as a kind of therapy and that it relaxed her, and she would later testify to that. The practice of keeping diaries was something Elaine continued right into her marriage with Bill.

In October 1977, Elaine and Tina were walking near the Charlie Company phone booths when two fellow soldiers sexually assaulted Elaine by grabbing her breast and buttocks.

Horrified by the event, Elaine informed Bill, who became incensed and searched the post for the two culprits. Once he found them, he beat them up, injuring his hand in the process. A couple days later, Tyree received orders to report to the 10th SFG (A) at Fort Devens in Ayer, Massachusetts. Elaine accompanied several people to the Richmond Airport to see him off. They made plans to see each other over the Thanksgiving holiday.

Bill Tyree arrived in Massachusetts by plane at Logan International Airport. He states, "That entire day of October 27, 1977, should have been an omen of things to come. I got off the plane at Logan Airport and walked into the main concourse, where I saw two men in blue uniforms with motorcycle knee high 'jack boots' and wearing parkas. Across the chest was a strap and they had their hats pulled down on the sides. Their uniforms looked similar to the uniform of the 1939 Gestapo, but blue instead of black. As I stared at them, I made the statement, 'You guys airport security?' I was looking for directions and it seemed like an appropriate question. In the wink of an eye, they both wheeled around to the left where I was standing in a US Army dress green uniform, pants bloused into a pair of spit shined jump boots, and a green beret. As they stepped within two feet of me, they asked where I was going. Was I employed? And did I have a photo ID? As I stood there looking at these two rocket scientists, it occurred to me that they were serious. When they were finished giving me the third degree, they returned my ID card and stated, 'We are Massachusetts State Police Officers!' I really didn't know whether I should bow or give them my loose change. I mean, these guys were truly full of themselves and that should've told me to run like hell."

Ayer, Massachusetts is located approximately fifty minutes from Boston. It is typical of a New England town, with quaint shops and restaurants along Main Street. It is the kind of place you have probably seen a hundred times in a postcard, where people say hello as they pass each other on the street. The main employer of the town is the United States Army post named Fort Devens, which is located on the outskirts of the town. Prior to its deactivation in 1996, it was the oldest US Army post in the country. It is not unusual for army personnel to be seen shopping in the stores or military equipment being transported through the town streets. Ayer has been a military town since World War I.

Fort Devens has been a major training and induction post for almost a hundred years. The post is so large that it has training and firing ranges on a separate South Post Annex across from Route 2 along with Moore Army Airfield that is located in the northeast section of Ayer, with the main post sitting in between the two. In June 1968, Military Intelligence built a mock Vietnamese village on the post and staffed it with members of the Menehune platoon from Company A of the Army Security Agency Training Regiment. These men were of Hawaiian descent and were brought to Fort

Devens to play Viet Cong at the Tactical Training Center. There also were Vietnamese mountain people who were recruited by the CIA to help fight communist insurgency into South Vietnam. The village was set up to train Army Intelligence officers on the proper procedures in dealing with the villagers. At the same time, the army was training the Menehune in US Army tactics.

After the Vietnam War, the main units attached to the post were Combat Support Battalion (Provisional). This unit was organized in 1980 and was composed of Headquarters and Headquarters Detachment, the 104th Transportation Company, the 278th General Supply Company, the 382nd Personnel Service Company, the 624th Military Police Company, the 642nd Engineer Company, and the 14th Explosive Ordnance Detachment. These groups were mainly in charge of housekeeping services for the post. That is to say that they acted as support for the other units on post. The other units on post receiving these support services were the 18th Army Band, the 39th Engineer Battalion (Combat), the 36th Medical Battalion, the Army Readiness and Mobilization Region I, the Army Intelligence School, and the 10th Special Forces Group (Airborne).

The 10th Special Forces Group (Airborne) is a direct descendant of the 4th Company 1st Regiment of the Joint American-Canadian 1st Special Service Force. The group was activated on June 19, 1952, at Fort Bragg, North Carolina with Colonel Aaron Bank in command. Headquarters and Headquarters Company, 10th SFG was activated on May 19, 1952, preceding the activation of the Group proper at Fort Bragg, NC, and in September 1953, following intensive individual and team training, 782 members of the 10th SFG deployed to Germany and established Group headquarters at Bad Tölz and Lenggries in Bavaria. In 1968, the majority of the Group redeployed to Fort Devens, Massachusetts. The 1st Battalion remained in Germany as part of Special

Forces Detachment Europe and is currently located at Panzer Kaserne in Stuttgart. Between 1994 and 1995, the 10th SFG moved to Fort Carson, Colorado, where three line battalions, 2nd, 3rd, and 4th, plus a Group Support Battalion, operate today.

The mission of the 10th Group is threefold:

1. Unconventional warfare (UW), required to provide personnel capable of organizing, training, and directing indigenous forces in the conduct of unconventional warfare operations within enemy occupied areas.

2. Foreign internal defense (FID), group stability operations. To accomplish this, the unit must be able to advise, assist, and train host country military and paramilitary forces in civil affairs, medical skills, psychological operations, engineering, sanitation techniques, and many other related subjects.

3. Direct action (DA) missions. Part of the group's mission is to provide personnel in a continuous state of readiness for highly sensitive missions of short duration strikes used to seize, capture, recover, or destroy enemy material, or recover personnel.

The subordinate units that make up the 10th Special Forces Group (A) located at Fort Devens were Headquarters and Headquarters Company, 2nd and 3rd Special Forces Battalion, Service Company, Signal Company, and the 10th Military Intelligence Company. The line battalions provide the muscle of the Group and consist of a Headquarters Detachment and three line companies. Each company comprises headquarters elements and five Special Forces Operational Detachments (SFODs). At the time when Bill was in the 1st SFG(A), they had up to thirty Special Forces

Operational Detachment Alphas, otherwise referred to as ODAs, at any given time. The SFODs are the backbone and basic operating element of the Group. Each SFOD consists of two officers—a captain and a lieutenant—and ten highly trained senior NCO specialists in operations and intelligence, light and heavy weapons, demolitions, communications, and military medicine. Each SFOD has the capability to organize, train, advise, and administer a 1500-man indigenous force engaged in the conduct of all types of unconventional warfare organizations.

The Army Intelligence School can trace its roots back to cryptologic training for army personnel that began in 1941 at Fort Monmouth, New Jersey. In 1945, with the establishment of the Army Security Agency, responsibility for cryptologic training was transferred to ASA. The school was relocated to Fort Devens, Massachusetts in 1951. On December 19, 1957, it was officially designated as the US Army Security Agency Training Center and School. On October 1, 1976, the US Army Security Agency Training Center and School became the US Army Intelligence School Fort Devens. The school is housed in an academic plant of forty buildings that provide 110 classrooms. Its mission is to provide programs of education and training for selected commissioned officers, warrant officers, enlisted personnel, noncommissioned officers, and civilians of all military services in command, staff management, administrative, supervisory, technical, operational, and maintenance areas of knowledge and skill. The USAIDS School Brigade provides command, control, administrative and logistics support to personnel assigned and attached to USAIDS. The School Brigade is responsible for the housing, feeding, health, welfare, morale, and non-technical training of students, staff, and faculty. This institution maintains a complex, diversified, and expanding curriculum devoted to fostering electronic warfare, electromagnetic and signal security skills on behalf of the intelligence community.

These two units, the 10th Special Forces Group (A) and the United States Army Intelligence School, seem to work independently of the rest of the base due to the sensitive nature of their missions and not all personnel have the same security clearance.

Bill arrived at Fort Devens on October 27, 1977, and was overcome by fever upon his arrival. The fever was caused by an infection in his right hand where he had been bitten by one of Elaine's assailants during the fight a few days earlier. After checking in with the 10th SFG, Tyree headed to the post hospital where he collapsed in the emergency room and wouldn't regain consciousness for thirty-six hours.

While in Cutler Army Hospital, Tyree convinced a nurse to bring a telephone into his room. He then called Elaine and proposed to her. Elaine accepted the proposal and they planned on a Christmas wedding at her family home in Cumberland, Maryland.

Bill recalls, "I called Elaine and asked her to marry me. It took her at least thirty seconds to make up her mind. She accepted and was coming for a visit at Thanksgiving."

Approximately a month later, Elaine came to Fort Devens to visit Bill. The two of them were once again inseparable all weekend long. They stayed in his barracks room while his roommates were off visiting family.

Bill states, "Elaine flew into Logan Airport and I went to pick her up with a guy from the unit that knew how to get in and around the area near the airport. Elaine spent four days in a barracks with three hundred troops. I shared a room with two other guys. That weekend we had the room to ourselves. The shower arrangement was a little more complicated, but Elaine wasn't a Girl Scout and giggled through the whole process. She was in a co-ed company at Fort Lee. There wasn't that much difference. Besides, as Elaine pointed out, if they want to look, they have to take their clothes off. 'It's a mutual thing,' she said. Elaine was readily accepted by the guys I ran with. They all thought she was out of her mind. Elaine was out there." At the conclusion of their weekend together, Elaine returned to her post and Bill was deployed and sent to Camp Riley, Minnesota for winter warfare training with the 2nd Battalion.

On December 31,1977, at a small church near Cumberland, Maryland near Elaine's home, Bill and Elaine tied the knot. Elaine wore a cream-colored dress and Bill was in his Class A dress green uniform, spit shined jump boots, and green beret. In attendance were most of Elaine's relatives and a few friends.

Bill fondly recalls, "We were married in a small chapel one block from her family home, just a small gathering." The honeymoon was short-lived as Bill had only a few days' leave before having to return to Fort Devens.

The 10th SFG was participating in the New England Winter Warfare Games, code named "Empire Glacier," in January 1978. Westover Air Force Base, MA was being used as the staging area. A confrontation broke out between Earl Michael Peters, a truck driver assigned to the 10th SFG and an African American soldier from the 18th Airborne Corps who was nonairborne qualified. Peters was armed with a buck knife while the other soldier had a straight razor. Bill and his immediate supervisor were able to diffuse the situation, and he and Peters subsequently become good friends. Earl Michael Peters stood about six feet, with a lanky build and dark hair. He was from Pennsylvania and had been in the army for a couple years. He acted like he was an innocent country boy who just liked to hunt and fish. In fact, he fancied himself as a kind of woodsman. However, his persona couldn't be further from the truth. He was a sneaky and vindictive person by all accounts and had a very dark side that few knew of.

In February 1978, a crippling blizzard struck the northeast, causing most of New England to be shut down for two weeks. The snow drifts around Fort Devens were as high as two and three stories in some areas. At the barracks of the 10th SFG, several soldiers, including Bill, began airborne operations by jumping off the roof of the three-story cement barracks into the two-story snow drifts. The post MPs arrived and informed the first sergeant to stop the men from jumping off the roof. The first sergeant replied, "Do it yourselves." The MPs left, scared they would be thrown off the roof if they approached the men.

Elaine was finally transferred from Fort Lee, Virginia to Fort Devens, Massachusetts. She was assigned to garrison and warned to stay away from the Green Berets because they were considered crazy by post personnel. Elaine informed them that she was married to a Green Beret. After only a week on post, she attended the Special Forces Association Valentines Dance with Bill and Master Sgt. "Odd Job" Makalena and his wife. Bill recalls, "Elaine grew closer to all the guys in my circle of friends except for Earl Michael Peters. She and Peters had words on several occasions. It had actually gotten so bad that I only saw him at work or around Fort Devens."

Elaine and Bill finally found an apartment at 24 Columbus Street in Ayer. Apartments were at a premium due to the proximity of the post to the town of Ayer. Menzie, Garcy, and Peters all helped Bill move himself and his new bride into a third-floor apartment that lacked the modern conveniences of other apartments. Bill fondly recalls, "That's where we fought the cockroaches for control of the open spaces. It was touch and go the entire time we lived there. I found out that Elaine was a clean freak. She cleaned everything, and sometimes she did it twice for good measure."

One evening in March 1978, Elaine and Bill were in their apartment watching television when someone knocked at the door. Elaine answered it and Peters and Peterson, fellow soldiers and friends of Bill's, asked if Bill was at home. Elaine ushered them in. They informed Bill that they needed his help as some of their friends had been in a bad fight at Stanley's Nightclub in Shirley on Route 2, owned by Stanley McNiff. The club was frequented by the younger soldiers at Fort Devens.

Bill, Peters, and Peterson left the apartment and drove to Fort Devens in Peterson's car. Once in the company area, Bill spoke to a few other men. Within twenty minutes, he and thirty-five fellow soldiers, one of them Dennis Testagrossa who was also from their unit, were outside the nightclub. Bill briefed the men and implemented his plan. He used a star cluster flare to blow out the window in the front of the club at the same time the thirty-five men rushed into the bar, and a large fist fight ensued. Bill and two other soldiers were arrested for "disorderly conduct." Bill was bailed out and the CID began investigating the incident. Bill was well liked by the men in his unit and they were loyal to one another no matter what the consequences were.

On an afternoon shortly after the aforementioned events, Elaine told Bill that she was six weeks pregnant. Almost immediately, Bill ran the truck into a dumpster. There was no damage to the truck or the dumpster, but he was in shock and excited.

A company formation was called on April 8, 1978. Tyree and four other soldiers were summoned in front of the formation, where the company commander pinned on the new rank of Spec 4. This was the second time Bill was promoted to Spec 4, the first time being during his first enlistment. After the promotions, the company was dismissed. Bill was on cloud nine. His new promotion meant a pay raise and with a baby on the way, it couldn't have come at a better time.

"No trooper, no special forces operative wants to sit behind a desk. We joined up to kick some doors down." Ant Middleton

CHAPTER TWO

Decent Into the Deep State

In early May 1978, Bill entered the 10th SFG headquarters. Coming out was Colonel Edward P. Cutolo, the man who had been in charge of Operation Watchtower in Panama during the months of February and March 1976. Bill saluted first then recognized him, and they started to converse. Colonel Cutolo told Bill to drop by group headquarters the first week in June, because an operation was being mounted in the New England area. He informed Bill that he was relieving Colonel Othar Shalikashvili of command of the 10th Special Forces Group. Colonel Shalikashvili was the older brother of General John Shalikashvili, Chairman of the Joint Chiefs of Staff under President Bill Clinton.

Colonel Edward Cutolo was a graduate of West Point class of 1954. While he was a cadet, he took Spanish language classes which he later used in Latin America. After graduation, he was sent to Fort Benning for Junior Officer Training, Parachute School, and finally, Ranger School. Next, he was assigned to the 11th Airborne, then headquarters, Strike Command, and then a year with the Vietnamese Army. By 1965, he was at the Command and Staff College at Fort Leavenworth. Upon graduation, he was sent to Argentina and later Venezuela due to his proficiency in Spanish. He was once again sent to Vietnam for battalion command in the 9th Infantry Division. It was here that he earned a Silver Star, Distinguished Flying Cross, three

Bronze Stars for Valor, and sixteen Air Medals, among other decorations. In 1970, he was sent to Fort Polk to take command of the Training Battalion, where he remained until he was selected to attend the Naval War College. While in Maryland, he also earned a master's degree in international affairs from George Washington University. Upon completion of his studies, Cutolo was selected for assignments in the office of the Deputy Chief of Staff for Operations, Department of the Army, and several classified missions. Now here he was, assigned to take over command of the 10th Special Forces Group (A) at Fort Devens.

Seeing Colonel Cutolo brought back a flood of memories for Bill. He had first met the colonel during his first enlistment. Colonel Cutolo was liked by the men under his command and was seen as someone whose star was on the rise.

Bill thought back to December of 1975. While stationed at Fort Bragg, he had been summoned to the orderly room of Headquarters Troop 1st / 17th Air Cavalry. When Bill walked into the room, he was ordered to report to Squadron Headquarters. He left and entered Squadron HQ to report to an SGM, who instructed him to report to the Green Ramp area of Pope Air Force Base, which was located adjacent to Fort Bragg. The Green Ramp Area was a staging area used for the mass deployment of troops from Fort Bragg, where they boarded a United States Air Force C-130 aircraft from which they would eventually jump when they were over the drop zone. The C-130, known as the work horse of the US Air Force, is also used to transport supplies and passengers. Upon his arrival at the Green Ramp Area, Bill reported to a small building on the outskirts of the Green Ramp. He saluted the two men in the office and once the salute was returned, he was told to board the C-130 taxiing approximately fifty yards from him with some two dozen other troops.

Bill approached the small group waiting to board the plane. Some of the men waiting with him seemed to know each other, although not much was being said. They walked up the ramp into the cavernous cargo plane and took seats on either side. The C-130 lifted off and a couple hours later, it landed at Eglin Air Force Base in Florida. The troops stayed onboard while the plane refueled and prepped for takeoff again. The next leg of the journey had the plane landing at the Military School of Aviation Forces in Honduras. When the plane landed this time, four Spanish officers boarded the aircraft. Then the plane again took off and landed a few hours later at Albrook Air Station in Panama.

Albrook Air Station was originally an American Air Force base. In 1975, the installation was downgraded to an Air Force station. The runway and control tower were closed, and the aircraft, units, and personnel were transferred to Howard Air Force Base. The installation was eventually turned over to the Panamanian government on October 1, 1979.

When the troops disembarked the plane, they were directed to a small building and tents in which they would be quartered. Bill received his assignment as a crew chief to a helicopter, UH-1, and was given a limited briefing as to his duties. As Bill and the rest of the men stood in formation, they were addressed by a well-built man with a naval anchor tattoo on his arm. Bill immediately identified this man as a Navy Seal. The man informed them that they would be in Panama for ten to fourteen days on a routine training exercise. They would be assigned to a helicopter and their job would be the same as if they were at Fort Bragg. "The Spanish officers we picked up are on an operation and we are to assist them in whatever they request. This operation is classified, and you're not to discuss it with anyone, not even anyone involved in it unless you have a mission-related reason for doing so." He then proceeded to march the men over to a nondescript building to sign military NDAs.

Bill and one other man decided to go out on the tarmac and check the UH-1 helicopters they would be flying in. As he checked out his helicopter, Bill immediately noticed a secure radio with cryptograph capability. This type of radio is not standard equipment in the helicopters at Fort Bragg. Then he noticed the mounts on the door were for twin M 60-D models and that there were no nomenclature plates anywhere allowing the aircraft to be identified as US Army property. The helicopters had been stripped of all identifiable markings, right down to the two 212 Pratt & Whitney engines that powered the helicopter.

Later that night, Bill sat in on a limited briefing. He was told that they had been tasked with delivering three Special Action Teams (SATs) to the border of Panama and Colombia. Since there were ongoing guerilla activities and hostilities in the area of operations, they would be flying hot, live ammo and everything. This would be treated as a real combat situation; nothing would be taken for granted. The two helicopters flew the SATs to the border and after the teams disembarked, both helicopters redeployed to a location 500 meters from the border to land. The helicopters would remain in a defensive position until the teams returned and would board the helicopters for redeployment to this staging area.

Early the next morning Bill rose, got dressed, and made his way with the other soldiers to a makeshift chow hall for breakfast. After a quick bite, the men moved *en masse* to the awaiting helicopters. The armed soldiers were on the tarmac, checking their equipment one last time before boarding the helicopters. Bill completed his own equipment check and did a routine walk around of the bird he was assigned to. Soon after, the pilots gave the signal to mount up and board. The helicopters lifted off and began the trip. They flew at an altitude that allowed them to skim the canopy of the jungle below all the while avoiding radar detection. The pilots maintained radio silence as the birds flew south.

The two helicopters touched down after a while and eighteen to twenty armed soldiers disembarked and scrambled into the jungle. After a radio check, the helicopters lifted off from the landing zone and went 500 meters north and landed. The pilots immediately exited the helicopters and began setting out Claymore mines, small motion detectors used to secure the perimeter. They stayed at the location for twenty-four days on constant alert. Fields of fire were established and watches were posted. Eight hours on, eight hours off; sleep was fleeting.

One night, while waiting to go and pick up the soldiers they had dropped off, Bill enquired about what exactly they were doing on this mission. The soldier next to him said, "Tyree. Let me tell you what you don't know. In the universe that you belong to, there are only big dogs. The dogs are so big that when they piss you think it's raining down here!"

Bill later recalled, "That was the general attitude of the officers that were involved in these operations. They knew they were made men. That their careers were assured strictly because they made it onto the playing field and could impress those that called the shots at the next level. Whatever was occurring at that time, I was not privy to."

During this time, thirty-seven cargo fixed-wing aircraft flew over their position heading north. The radio call came in, the men quickly tore down the temporary encampment, and the two helicopters headed for the landing zone. The troops set off yellow and green smoke grenades to signal their position to the helicopters. Once the troops boarded the helicopters, they headed to refuel and then to Albrook Air Station. When they landed, Bill saw the fixed-wing aircraft he had seen flying overhead earlier. Panamanian National

Guard soldiers were unloading bales from the planes and placing them in a building with only one entrance; a Colonel Noriega was overseeing the operation. Twenty-five minutes later, Bill and the rest of the United States soldiers were heading back to MacDill Air Force Base in Florida.

In February 1976, Bill was once again selected to head to Panama. This time, while the two helicopters were waiting in the middle of the jungle, the pilot got off the radio and told the crews to mount up, the home team had casualties. At the landing zone, SAT members carried two wounded members aboard and one soldier informed Bill to look in a certain area, adding, "If they come, you shoot." Well, they came. Bill fired on three heavily armed men, killing one man for certain. As that man took a direct burst from the twin Delta M-60's machine guns in the chest, the other two men went down but crawled off into the bush. One casualty was hit in the chest, the other in the thigh. The helicopters headed for the refueling area, where they unloaded the wounded directly onto a US Army Med-Evac.

When the helicopters landed at Albrook, Colonel Cutolo commanded, "All SAT personnel report immediately for debriefing. Air crews, break down the equipment and clean it up. Debriefing for air crews will be in three hours. The quarantine remains in effect." Bill overheard that the SAT members had been mistaken for guerillas by the Colombian Army, and a fire fight had ensued.

After the briefing, Colonel Cutolo requested that Bill report to him. He told him to stay out of the way of the old timers. During this meeting, Bill didn't know that Cutolo was a colonel in the US Army. He was under the impression that he was an advisor. After the meeting, Bill began to question what was going on. Later that evening, while being restricted to quarters like everybody else, he snuck out and into the building housing the bales. He managed to gain entry into the building without being noticed, broke open a bale, and got a piece of what looked like white chalk. He later learned that this was pure cocaine, but that was all he was able to learn.

Bill recalls, "I witnessed the cocaine off loaded from the aircraft and stacked on the tarmac at Albrook Air Station. The stacks varied in size but averaged ten to fifteen feet wide, ten to twelve feet high, and twenty to twenty-five feet long. The stacks consisted of bales of cocaine that would be as small as a hard bound dictionary, and as large as a bundle of hay. I saw Colonel Noriega touring the area and standing next to the cocaine on the tarmac. Colonel Noriega was in charge of the Panamanian Intelligence and Customs section of the National Guard. The bales were being flown in by plane and met by Colonel Noriega and others, after which the cocaine was housed in a building located at one end of the tarmac/runway."

The next mission was in March 1976. This was the mission that went drastically wrong. The Home Team was compromised near the border. Colombian Army soldiers on patrol in the jungle stumbled across the SAT team. Since the SAT team members weren't wearing any insignias on their uniforms, they were mistaken for guerillas. A severe fire fight ensued and the SAT team, realizing the severity of the situation, called for an extraction. The helicopters flew into Colombia and picked up the SAT team at the LZ (landing zone). The teams were quickly loaded onto the helicopters and they made their way back toward Panama. The helicopters were met in Panamanian air space by a US Army AH-1 Attack "Cobra" helicopter. Once back at Albrook Air Station, all personnel were debriefed. The men were then loaded onto a C-130 and headed back to their duty stations in the United States.

Once Bill returned to Fort Bragg, he went back to work as a door gunner. Some of his friends questioned where he had been. Remembering the confidentiality papers he had signed, he just gave a standard reply of TDY training. This seemed to appease his friends, at least for the time being.

Bill states that in July 1976, he was selected for Project Sandman, which allegedly was a Central Intelligence Agency operation. A seven-man wet operation team, along with Bill, arrived by helicopter in an unknown Central American country. The orders were to kill two communist military officers as they ate breakfast with their wives. Five members of the hit team were to secure the perimeter while the other two would act as a sniper team and take the shot. After the assassination, the team was ambushed while making its way back to the extraction point. The team radioed for a helicopter, which arrived in minutes. The team was extracted and Bill met Colonel Carone, who was on the helicopter. Bill and the other six members of the team found themselves back in the United States hours later.

Bill had never discussed with anyone the events that he had taken part in during his first enlistment. Now Colonel Cutolo was back in his life, and he couldn't help but wonder what was going to be asked of him next.

During the month of May 1978, Bill further learned that he had been selected as Soldier of the Month for the 10th SFG and was a candidate for Soldier of the Quarter. The first sergeant presented him with a coin. This is a very high honor to be selected for and to be in the running for Soldier of the Quarter was unbelievable.

According to Bill, he met with Colonel Cutolo in his office during the first week of June 1978. During that meeting, Bill was asked if he would like to participate in a new operation that was being assembled, nicknamed Operation Orwell. Bill would be assigned to a surveillance team that would monitor public, political, and religious officials, pursuant to Army Regulation (AR) 340-18-5, file number 503-505. The next night, the team was briefed,

"It's necessary to keep prominent state and federal judicial, legislative, and executive governmental officials under surveillance to determine if anyone has heard anything about Operation Watchtower, so the army can take precautionary steps and contain the damage."

An hour later, Bill found himself in a nondescript van packed with electronic surveillance equipment, parked outside the mayor's house on a quiet street in Lunenburg, Massachusetts. A three-member SAT team was about to enter the home and check the equipment that had malfunctioned when one member slipped on ice while exiting the vehicle and injured his arm. They helped the injured man into the van and finished their mission.

The next mission was in late June to early July 1978. The SAT team, including Bill, was outside the private residence of Middlesex County District Attorney John Droney. The team turned on their surveillance equipment once they were in position and began to hear what sounded like adults engaged in relations. The team quickly realized that this was not a typical tryst. At that moment, Droney was engaged in homosexual activity with his lover, according to Bill. Once they were finished, the two men began to talk and Droney admitted to covering up the murder of an escaped felon named Edgar W. Cook by the Cambridge Police in the early 1960s. Cook allegedly committed suicide when police raided the apartment he was hiding in. Then Droney detailed how he had engineered a theft of $240,000 from the mayor of Somerville.

According to Bill, "In 1962, the mayor of Somerville received a federal grant for $240,000. The money was located in a small, black floor safe located within the office of the mayor." Droney further stated that he had "arranged for that money to be stolen from the safe. The money was taken in the night while a guard stood just outside the door of the mayor's office. The office had a private bathroom and two windows. A Somerville Police officer had committed the theft by climbing up the scaffolding that was in place for renovations on City Hall and the high school, entering through a window and opening the safe using the combination that was under the blotter on the mayor's desk." The SAT team recorded and photographed what they could and brought their findings back to Fort Devens.

During this time, Elaine was growing increasingly aggravated with the odd hours Bill was working because of his new assignment with the SAT team. Still under the impression that her husband worked at FST as supply personnel, she had no knowledge of his participation in the surveillance.

Bill had been what the military calls "full flash qualified," a fact substantiated by several other full flash qualified Special Forces Qualified Green Berets, while disputed by others. This meant that he had enough training and taken special courses to be classified as a qualified Green Beret even though he had not attended the Special Forces Qualification Course. The flash was the insignia on the green beret. Since at that time, a Special Forces unit allowed all personnel to wear a green beret with their uniform, the unit designated color flash on the beret. However, in order to denote who was a Special Forces qualified soldier from those soldiers who were just working to support the unit, they wore a quarter-inch bar under the unit crest to denote their status as unqualified. Bill was stripped of his full flash when David L. Peterson, a man he associated with, was placed under arrest. The group commander, Colonel Cutolo, did this because he had the authority to do so; today it takes a general officer. When Bill was stripped of his full flash, Colonel Cutolo didn't have any evidence at all that Bill was engaging in criminal behavior with Peterson. This punishment was doled out because the two men occasionally hung out together on post.

After a long talk, Bill understood Elaine's point of view and decided to request reassignment. After all, he would soon be the proud father of a new baby and he would need to be around the apartment more to help out.

In mid-July, Bill walked into headquarters and asked Colonel Cutolo to be reassigned off the surveillance team. The request was denied and he was warned to stay silent about the surveillance operation. Bill states, "When I attempted to get out of Operation Orwell, I was served with notice that the CID would be brought to bear and I would conform and stay with the program or be run over by it!"

Around this time, Bill was reassigned to the 441st Military Intelligence Detachment (MID) from FST. He reported to Captain James Williams, Commanding Officer, and was assigned a job that encompassed several different jobs, including finance NCO, supply sergeant, and CBR NCO.

By late July, Tyree felt that maybe he should give it another shot at getting reassigned from surveillance. He again appeared in Colonel Cutolo's office to request reassignment. Cutolo ordered Bill to report to the Fort Devens Mental Health Outpatient Clinic for evaluation. Tyree was taken aback by the order but complied and was evaluated by the staff at the clinic. The staff rendered a report that stated Tyree was in perfect mental health and there was no reason for him to be interviewed again.

A week later, Tyree received an order to report to the Criminal Investigation Division (CID) office. When he arrived, he was read his rights and informed that he had been identified and accused by Erik Aarhus, a supply clerk in the parachute riggers shed, of selling Aarhus a rope belonging to the army. Tyree denied the accusation and refused to answer any CID questions.

Captain Daniel Carrigan was assigned to represent Tyree. Agent Joe Burzynski was then informed that Tyree wouldn't answer any questions. Tyree and Carrigan left the CID office and headed back to their respective offices. Bill quickly thought back to the veiled threat that Colonel Cutolo had made to him when he requested reassignment from the surveillance team. He now realized that Colonel Cutolo was going to use trumped up charges from the CID to discredit him if he had any notion of mentioning the surveillance teams.

Bill recalls, "Colonel Cutolo ordered that I remain assigned to the 441st MID. This in itself was unusual, as a soldier pending a court-martial is not supposed to be assigned to any area that is deemed sensitive or which contains classified material The 441st MID was the only Military Intelligence Detachment for the entire 10th SFG. The 441st MID was a sensitive area due to the classified materials, which were stored in the various vaults within the single level structure that housed the 441st MID."

Typical of army posts during this time, there was an ever-growing drug problem among the ranks. This was a bad time for the United States Army. It was post-Vietnam, and the army was not getting a high caliber of personnel; some soldiers had even enlisted in an attempt to avoid serving jail time. Fort Devens was no exception, and adding to the problem was that the post was open, meaning civilian automobiles could cut through the area to access the civilian community on the other side of Fort Devens. The military police on any of the gates weren't ensuring that only military personnel or visitors having military business were allowed on post due to the post being open. This allowed many unsavory individuals to gain access to military personnel. Also during this time, the CID was investigating a rash of thefts of military property from all over the post. The biggest theft occurred at the 10th Special Forces Group

Forward Support Team Two. The missing equipment ranged from climbing rope to cold weather gear.

On August 1, 1978, Bill and Elaine moved into their new apartment at 104 ½ Washington Street in Ayer. This apartment was located on the first floor of a brick building located farther back from the road than other homes in the area. An identical apartment building was located across the parking lot. Both buildings were rented to civilian and military personnel. Menzie, Peters, and Garcy helped Bill and Elaine move into their new apartment.

By mid-August, Bill checked in with his attorney, Captain Carrigan, at his office only to learn that he was under hack and would be tried by court-martial, facing military prison and a bad conduct discharge. Bill was in shock, but Carrigan assured him the charges would be dropped due to a lack of evidence.

A few days later, Elaine and Bill had Earl Michael Peters over for dinner as a thank you for his assistance in helping them move. During this dinner, Elaine learned that Peters had paid Dennis Testagrossa to steal his truck and destroy it because the payments were too high. The truck was taken from behind Carlins and driven out to Shirley, Massachusetts. Dennis drained the oil and ran the motor for about fifteen minutes before setting the vehicle on fire. This ensured that the vehicle would be a total loss. Elaine continued keeping a diary on the illegal activities she learned about on Fort Devens from her job at the Billeting Officers Quarters (BOQ) discussed in front of her, as well as the different military operations that Special Forces officers had been involved with since her arrival at Fort Devens. She wrote down everything, unaware of the secrecy level of much of the information.

***

While the CID continued investigating the theft of military property around Fort Devens, Earl Michael Peters was stealing patrolling caps from the FST 2 and selling them to the guys at the 10th SFG motor pool. Peters broke into the 10th SFG motor pool tool room by himself and stole several thousand dollars' worth of tools. Peters also had a partner in crime during this time. His name was David L. Peterson, and the two of them were stopped by the military police while on post. When their vehicle was searched, two star clusters were discovered and the men were arrested. Peters also stole a brush guard from Fitchburg Ford and sold it for $75.00. During 1978, the CID reported a record crime wave at Fort Devens, which they quickly attributed to either Bill, Peters, Peterson, or three other soldiers in SFG(A). The missing items went beyond gear, cameras, and fire extinguishers, eventually including at least two US Army 18-wheelers full of gear.

Erik Aarhus was considered kind of a loner by his fellow soldiers. He was not a very tall fellow, but he had a head full of brown hair and was always squared away when it came to his uniform. He had an ever-increasing drug habit that his superiors and fellow soldiers knew about but chose to ignore because it didn't interfere with his job performance. Erik, by his own admission, spent most of his time in the service in a drug-induced stupor, to the point he cannot remember much about his years in the military. One of his duties at the rigger shack was to drive the riggers from the main post to the airfield and back at the end of the day. He even had a homemade sign on his desk at the riggers shack, kind of a nameplate that said "Captain Beyond." This was his self-assigned nickname. He was also known as being someone who would do anything for a dollar.

Peters even sold Bill a .45 caliber US Army sidearm with seven rounds minus a clip. The worst thing that Peters did was to sell bad angel dust to a former roommate of his named Carrick, and to another soldier who punched him in the face at the 39th mess hall, knocking Peters out.

Bill recalls, "It all began in February of 1978. I was working at FST 2, when a Private David Peterson came there to work. At the time, Elaine and I were having a little trouble. We had been married for two months and she had just gotten to Fort Devens from Fort Lee, Virginia. Me and Peterson had become good friends and started going to Stanley's nightclub. I guess March is when it started to happen. I started to notice supply items we stocked were missing, and on different occasions started seeing these things in the company area such as patrol caps, ATA straps, smoke grenades, and other items. I heard through the company grapevine that Peterson was selling those items for a profit. I also had seen a set of bolt cutters in his care similar to the ones we had at FST, at least in size and color.

"At any rate, we had been at 1st Battalion C Company ASA one evening and he introduced me to a young lady named Jean Hackler. She was seeing someone else and he seemed to know her from Nebraska before she got to Fort Devens. He was mad at her about something and suggested we fix her wagon. Well, at that time—I should say a couple of days before—I had counted some star clusters and smoke grenades we had stored at the FST. Then the next day, I counted them and four star cluster flares and as many smoke grenades were missing. When I confronted him, he said that he would put me in the middle of it if I told SFC Mackalena. Then Peterson came to my home and asked for my help. Even with things like they were between us, I went with him. He, Sass, and Hines set off a total of about six star clusters in Heritage Square and they pointed them in the direction of Jean Hackler's window. After they discharged them, they threw them on top of A Company."

"We were all supposed to go to Stanley's nightclub and when we ran into Earl Peters, we invited him to come with us. Well, instead of heading in the direction of the night club, we began to head toward the 2500 section of post, in the vicinity of FST 2. About a block away, he told us that he had to run into FST and pick something up that he had forgotten. Well, this didn't sound right to me. So, I suggested that they drop me off and go to the Service Company motor pool and wait. I walked past the FST and I didn't see anybody. As I walked toward the service company area, I told Peterson that whatever he did, I didn't want to know about it."

"When he came back, he had a sandbag and he didn't tell us what was in it. The next day, it dawned on me that he had to have a set of keys to the FST since I still had my keys. Monday morning arrived and when we entered the FST, I opened up and noticed all the hand receipts were missing, and it appeared that someone had broken in through the upstairs window. When the questioning started, Peterson came and told me that the bag he left at my house contained the hand receipts and some star clusters, along with some smoke grenades. He had brought the bag into my apartment without me noticing and hid it in my bedroom in a wooden army footlocker that I had. Elaine thought the sandbag was mine and never questioned it.

"At this point, I knew I was deeply involved. He promised that if I helped him, he wouldn't say nothing to my wife and if caught he would involve Peters or me. So, I called a friend in the Signal Company and this was at 10:00 the morning of the break-in. I gave Peterson four dollars for a taxi and told him to get rid of the bag. So, he went to my apartment and let himself in with my key and left with the bag. On his way downstairs he met my wife. When I came home that evening, I told her everything about me and the events concerning the FST break-in." Bill distanced himself from Peterson after these events.

Bill was in a small way connected with some of the criminal activity that took place on post, just as many other soldiers had been. His connection came from knowledge after the fact. His superiors also knew exactly what everyone was involved with and they considered Bill's misdemeanors as a tool to be used against him if needed. Despite being under a BCD Special Court-Martial, Tyree was given a letter of commendation for preparing an extensive plan to deploy the twenty-two-man 441st MID anywhere in the world. The commendation included laudatory comments from the US Army Inspector General himself. The letter of commendation was given to Bill by Captain Jimmy W. Williams, Detachment Commander of the 441st MID, who curiously enough was a military police captain.

The letter of commendation raised several eyebrows in the 10th SFG(A). First, this was because of the BCD Special Court-Martial. Second, because like most of the other training Bill displayed, there was no record in his Army 201 personnel file of when or where he had received the training. Bill just knew things he shouldn't have known. His enlisted evaluation reports (EERs) actually mention that Bill had a vast knowledge of military matters befitting someone more senior in age and rank, but there is no mention of where that vast knowledge came from.

Around this same time, Ken Garcy, Bill, and Elaine were hanging out in the apartment at 104 ½ Washington Street, and Bill stepped out of the apartment. He was in the basement area putting some boxes away when the phone rang. Elaine answered and was horrified by what was being said to her on the other end. Immediately, Garcy jumped out of his seat, ripped the phone from Elaine, and began to threaten the caller. When Bill returned to the apartment, he was informed of the call and promised to take care of the situation.

The next day, Bill marched into 1SG Fred Henry's office and informed him of the threats he had received the night before and how they were upsetting to his wife and himself.

Henry reassured him that the problem would be looked into. Bill states, "By November 1978, we were getting verbal threats over the phone and written notes on the windshield. Once this was reported to my chain of command, I expected it to stop. It never did." At the time, Bill believed that the threats were to scare him silent about his involvement in past military operations.

Bill later recalls, "In 1978, unbeknownst to me, Elaine began to receive information about United States Army Special Forces soldiers at Fort Devens. She began to listen closer and document Operation Watchtower in her diary. When we began to receive death threats over the phone and in writing left on the windshield of our truck, I took action. I notified my chain of command within the 441st Military Intelligence Detachment, the 10th Special Forces Group Airborne Fort Devens. Nothing was done and the threats kept coming. I spoke to my father, a retired United States Army Non-Commissioned Officer, who contacted United States senator E.J. "Jake" Garn (R-Utah). Senator Garn was a powerful senator who sat on the United States Senate Armed Forces Service Committee. Normally, when a senator makes an official inquiry into the US Army through what is known as a Congressional Inquiry, the army jumps. This time the army didn't even yawn."

According to Senator Garn, "The first time I learned there were possible threats against Bill and Elaine Tyree was in December of 1978, upon receipt of the December 17, 1978, letter from Bill's parents. They expressed concern that Bill couldn't turn in evidence against some of his alleged friends who were also implicated in the theft of government property. Specifically, they stated, "There is a positive danger here. A danger to my son, daughter-in-law, and three-week-old granddaughter... At this point I am not sure that he has not been threatened; he would not admit it if he had been." After receipt of Tyree's parents' letter,

Senator Garn again wrote to the Department of the Army, Major G. James, Chief of Legislative Liaison, on January 12, 1979, and enclosed a copy of the December 17 letter. Senator Garn's letter requested that the army look into the matter and report back to him.

Prior to receipt of Tyree's parents' letter of December 17, 1978, Senator Garn received a report from the Department of the Army, Colonel Forrest Rittgers Jr., dated November 24, 1978. Senator Garn said, "This was in response to my inquiry to the army dated October 25, 1978, after receipt of Bill's letter to Senator Garn, which he received on October 17, 1978. Neither of these pieces of correspondence indicated any threat to life or danger, or the involvement of drugs and arms trafficking." Colonel Rittgers only indicated a charge of stealing and selling of government property. Bill's letter discussed the events that led to his being implicated in the theft, his clean record and promotion, and how he was being wrongfully accused for something he didn't do.

Senator Garn made written inquiries to the army on December 25, 1978, and on January 17, 1979, in response to Bill's letter and his parents' letter to him respectively. The army had not responded in writing to Senator Garn's January 12, 1979, inquiry which mentioned the threat to Bill's life and that of his wife. However, Garn's office did on January 29, 1979, receive a call from someone named Doucette from the army. The message left was that they (the army) received the latest inquiry and it would be two weeks before we would get an answer. The next contact was from Bill's mother by telephone regarding the tragic death of her daughter-in-law to Senator Garn.

Senator Garn didn't know for certain whether Colonel Forrest Rittgers knew of the threat to life prior to January 30, 1979, but there was sufficient time for him to be notified.

Senator Garn also had statements on record by Bill's father that he called Colonel Rittgers on January 18 and January 19, 1979, and told him that Bill and his wife had been receiving threatening telephone calls and requested Bill and Elaine be transferred for their safety. According to Senator Garn's notes of the first conversation, Colonel Rittgers said that he had not read through the report and promised to check with the provost marshal to post a patrolman around Bill's house.

As Senator Garn stated previously, he received a report from Colonel Rittgers on November 24, 1978, regarding Bill's court-martial proceedings. Again, on May 30, 1979, he received a report from Colonel Robert L. Simpson, Chief Assistance Division and Office of the Inspector General. It stated that the final action on Bill's appeal of the military justice proceedings had not been completed, but if he had any questions, he should check with Fort Devens Staff Judge Advocate General.

Senator Garn had no knowledge that Fort Devens had ever been investigated with respect to drug trafficking. It was Bill and his parents who mentioned books and diaries that Elaine had kept on illegal activities going on at Fort Devens. Sometime between January 31 and February 2, 1979, the senator's staff assistant was notified by a man, perhaps Colonel Moore or Major Garrett from the Army Liaison, that this case possibly involved arms and drug trafficking at Fort Devens. This was the first time that Senator Garn's office heard of this issue being introduced. While it was news to the regular army in Washington, DC, it was not news to the participants of Operation Watchtower. No mention of Watchtower ever made it to the ears of the army in Washington, DC.

Colonel Rittgers recalled the events surrounding Senator Garn. He states, "I know that Senator Garn and Congressman Marriott communicated with the army regarding the status of Tyree's larceny investigation. That correspondence was then routed to Fort Devens by the army's Office of Legislative Liaison (OCLL) for follow-up and reply. That type of thing was typically referred to the Fort Devens Inspector General for investigation and preparation of a response for my signature that would go to OCLL and then on to the originator. Tyree's father also communicated both to members of Congress (Garn and Marriott) and to Fort Devens directly. He called me on at least one occasion with respect to Tyree's larceny investigation and the type of disciplinary action contemplated. I have seen a statement purportedly written by him to the effect that he talked to me by phone regarding threats having been received by the Tyrees and that I promised to have their off-post apartment placed under surveillance. That is incorrect. At no time did he tell me of such threats, and I made no such promises of protection and/or surveillance. I have also seen a statement from Tyree's mother to the same effect. Again, not correct. I have no recollection of ever having talked with her."

On the early morning of November 23, 1978, Elaine and Bill went to Leominster-Fitchburg Hospital. Elaine gave birth at 6:45 p.m. to a 6 1/2-pound baby girl whom Bill named Dawn. Bill fondly recalls, "After the baby was born, Elaine was on maternity leave. I would drive in, walk into our ground level apartment, and she would simply say, 'Bill, talk to your daughter, she won't listen to me!' I'd take off my boots and fatigue blouse and sit in the rocking chair with the baby. We'd communicate with a series of slow or fast rocking motions of the chair. The fast motions she liked the best. They'd calm her down immediately. Sometimes, if Elaine had a truly bad day, I'd drive in, bundle the baby up in winter clothes, and we'd drive into the company area. Sometimes, guys would be coming or going on and off parachute jumps and training exercises. Here were these big, burly Green Berets with fifty pounds of equipment and they'd come to the common area where the charge of quarters would sit at. They'd see Dawn and go, 'Wow. A baby! Hey Bill, that your kid?' Of course, I would just shake my head yes and smile. They'd give her attention and she really liked that."

The week after the baby was born, Bill headed to Attorney Carrigan's office to discuss his BCD-CM. Carrigan informed him that Erik Aarhus had recently recanted his statement with the CID. Aarhus had entered the CID office on the morning of November 30, 1978. Carrigan presented Tyree with Aarhus's statement, which is as follows:

Q: Do you wish in any way to change the statement you made on 23 June 1978?

Aarhus: Yes.

Q: What happened when you talked to Peterson?

Aarhus: I guess Peterson has something against Tyree, but I for sure didn't. Peterson offered me $20 to make a statement against Tyree to say he sold me the rope. But I, myself, had a personal grudge against Tyree at that time.

Q: Did you accept the $20?

Aarhus: Yes, I did.

After Bill read these statements, among others, he breathed a sigh of relief, now knowing that the charges against him should be dropped.

Carrigan explained to Bill what exactly was going on with the CID investigation. Erik Aarhus, Frederick Owens, Steven Denton Jr., and Earl Michael Peters were all involved in this case. Aarhus had originally implicated Tyree by stating that he bought a rope from him, then he recanted his statement after a change of heart. Denton informed Carrigan that he was also approached by Peterson to write a statement implicating Bill but refused to comply. Peterson was implicated by several soldiers of selling stolen equipment and cold weather gear, while Peterson denied all knowledge in his statement to the CID.

CID agent Burzynski was the lead agent in the investigation against Tyree and responsible for forcing Aarhus to lie in his original statement. As all the events unfolded, there were two things that seasoned combat veterans in Special Forces mused about the threats made to Bill and Elaine Tyree. First, the reports of threats that made it all the way to Washington, DC, were not the conduct of either a thief or airborne soldier trying to conceal his position. One of the prime directives in the military is that if the enemy can find you because you gave away your position, you are dead. As a thief, the last thing you want is attention; it is harder to steal and fence that which you stole. The attention to the report of threats was out of character. Second, it was out of character unless Bill was not a thief, but a soldier concerned for the safety of his family. Then Bill wouldn't think twice about giving his position away, as his unknown enemy already knew where he and his family were at.

A Field Grade Article 15 is a non-judicial punishment under the Uniformed Code of Military Justice. The UCMJ is a set of laws set forth that all military personnel must adhere to while serving in the military. An Article 15 is usually administered by a commander with the rank of major or above. Through the use of this mechanism, the chain of command punishes a soldier for offenses under the UCMJ without formally charging the soldier at a court-martial proceeding. The average punishment usually consists of extra duty, restrictions, oral reprimand, or admonition.

Attorney Carrigan entered all the information from his investigation in Tyree's appeal of his Field Grade Article 15 proceeding to Colonel Rittgers, Post Commander.

According to the appeal of the punishment report that Captain Carrigan filed January 26, 1979, the following facts were stated: "SP4 Aarhus in his written statement indicated that he had purchased a rope from PVT Tyree. When I talked with him, he denied having done so, and stated that PV2 David Peterson paid him $20 to make this false allegation against PVT Tyree. PFC Denton told me that this same PV2 David Peterson was 'standing over his shoulder' while he (PFC Denton) was preparing a statement for his company commander regarding his knowledge of thefts from FST. Denton claims that Peterson tried to get him to say that he had seen Tyree sell a rope to another soldier in the FST and to write his statement so as to throw suspicion for the thefts from the FST upon Tyree. Denton said that he initially did as Peterson wanted, but tore it up and wrote another for the commander since the original was not true.

"PFC Earl Peters told me that he was at dinner at Tyree's home on the evening of the break-in at the FST. PV2 David Peterson was also present and Peters says that it was Peterson, not Tyree, who talked about going to the FST that night to do something about covering up the missing property. He said that the three of them left Tyree's house in Peterson's car, dropped Tyree off near the FST, and drove to the motor pool to check with CQ. When he came out a few minutes later, Tyree was walking up to the car with some personal gear in his hand. Tyree put the gear in the front seat and got into the car. Peterson then walked off toward the FST. He returned a short while later with a sandbag which appeared to be full and put it in the trunk. Neither Peterson nor Tyree said anything about having broken into the FST or having taken anything from it. Peters also told me that he had talked with three of Peterson's friends from ASA, Sass, Rudio, and Hines about a month or so after Peterson arrived at Fort Devens, who told him that they had bought certain cold weather equipment and mountain climbing gear from Peterson."

"The significance of the following lies in the fact that the principal witness against PVT Tyree and indeed, the catalyst for all actions against him, was PV2 David Peterson, who paid PVT Aarhus to make a false statement against PVT Tyree, the same PV2 Peterson who attempted to influence PFC Denton to say he had witnessed Tyree sell a rope when he had not. The same PV2 Peterson who, according to PVT Owens, sold him a star cluster and two smoke grenades in PVT Owen's room. The same PV2 Peterson who, according to PFC John P. Rudio's own statement, sold him snap links, pitons, a piton hammer, a snowsuit, and a pair of crampons. The same PV2 Peterson who came forward with his allegations and machinations against PVT Tyree only after being apprehended by the military police along with PFC Earl Peters in Peterson's car with munitions in his possession.

"With regard to the specific charges—the sale of property to Rudio—it is clear from Rudio's own statement that this sale was made by PVT2 David Peterson and not PVT Tyree. PFC Peters' statement referencing his conversation with Rudio also directly points to Peterson. Concerning the sale of property to Owens, whose statement indicated that once again the sale was made by Peterson, it should be noted that Owens had been discharged from the service under other than honorable conditions, and at the time he made his original statement he was under charges for an extended AWOL. He indicated to me that unless he made a statement implicating Tyree, the command would have pursued a court-martial instead of the administrative discharge. It should also be noted that PVT2 Peterson, in his sworn statement to the CID, denied ever being present at the sale to Owens, contrary to Owens' original statement to the CID. The break in at the FST, PVT Peters' statements to myself, CPT Carey, and CPT Houpe indicated that it was Peterson, not Tyree, who talked about breaking into 2nd BN FST to cover up thefts by stealing the hand receipts while at Tyree's house, that it was Peterson, not Tyree, who went back from the motor pool to the 2nd BN FST and returned with the sandbag full of hand receipts and pyrotechnics. Peters' first statement was made shortly after he and Peterson had been apprehended by the military police with certain pyrotechnics in Peterson's car.

"Peters said nothing about Tyree talking about a break-in. I respectfully submit that the only witness as to the charges against PVT Tyree, who was either not under some sort of cloud himself (i.e. Owens, Peters, Peterson himself), not approached by PVT2 Peterson to lie about PVT Tyree (Aarhus, Denton), or who was not, at the time his statement was taken, easily accessible to PVT2 Peterson (Sass, Hines), was PFC Rudio, and he specifically says that he bought gear from PVT2 Peterson. Until these incidents and indeed, since then, he has had not only a good but an outstanding military record."

Owens' own testimony admits that his discharge helps corroborate Bill's claims that Army CID agent Burzynski would be prosecuting him in an effort to discredit him because of his request to be reassigned from Operation Orwell.

By mid-December, Elaine, Bill, and Dawn went to an appointment at Captain Carrigan's office. Bill was informed that the government was offering him an Article 15. Bill said he would have to consider the offer and in the meantime, he and his wife would like to have some wills drawn up since they were parents now.

A few weeks later, Bill, Elaine, Dawn, and Peters were shopping at the Burlington Mall. Peters went into Herman's Sporting Goods Store and purchased a Remington 1100

12-gauge automatic shotgun. When they arrived back in Ayer at the Tyrees' apartment, the shotgun was broken down into two pieces and placed in the storage compartment under their couch. This was so Peters wouldn't have to go through the hassle of checking the weapon in at the arms room. Then Bill drove Peters back to the 10th SFG Service Company barracks.

Elaine continued working at the Bachelor Officer Quarters on post. According to Bill, on the night before Elaine was killed, he was reading her diaries about the criminal activities at Fort Devens. He said Elaine had written about how she walked into First Lieutenant John Klein's room in the course of performing her job and witnessed the officer burning stolen target folders from the 441st Military Intelligence Detachment. According to Bill, Lieutenant Klein was being investigated for stealing target folders from the 3rd Battalion 10th SFG(A), which contained targets in Eastern Europe under the control of the Communists and selling them to the Russians. Once this was discovered, the army sent First Lieutenant Klein to a Veterans Administration Hospital in Bedford, Massachusetts and from there they were able to contain the incident.

Bill recalls the night before Elaine was killed, "I returned to our off-post apartment late in the evening and found Elaine writing in her diaries. Elaine acted unusual and that caused me to take the diaries from her and read them for the first time ever. Inside the diaries I found nothing but entries related to illegal activities in and around Fort Devens. I also found mention of Operation Orwell and the surveillance that was underway at that time. I threw the diaries on the kitchen table next to where Elaine was standing and told her to get the diaries out of the apartment. At that time, I understood what the threatening phone calls had meant."

On January 5, 1979, Colonel Cutolo ordered Bill to report to his office. Once at the 10th SFG (A) headquarters, he reported to a sergeant and was informed that it was in his best interest to accept the Article 15, or his army career would be over. Bill agreed to the ultimatum and signed the Article 15. He was then ordered to wait outside Colonel Cutolo's office.

Aarhus and Peterson were next to enter the office. Once they left, Bill was called back in and given a non-judicial punishment and a reduction of all rank. Bill drove home in disgust to see Elaine. None of the crimes Bill had committed were what he was being accused of or punished for. It was all a set up. Bill was now seeing the military that he so admired without rose-colored glasses, and he quickly became disillusioned by it.

Elaine's enlistment was coming to an end, due to the birth of Dawn. She was due to muster out of the army by the end of January 1979. She and Bill decided that since she was leaving the army and they would be losing her life insurance policy, they should get some new policies as they now had a daughter There were also many late-night conversations about whether she would stay with Bill in Ayer or take Dawn to Utah and stay with Bill's family. They finally agreed that Elaine would stay in Ayer with Bill. He now recalls that a lot of Special Forces guys who had been involved in questionable activity seemed to have a lot of bad luck after his Article 15. He received mail asking him if they were mentioned in the diaries because they had spoken to Elaine.

"Gentlemen, prepare to defend yourself."
Sergeant Major Basil Plumley

CHAPTER THREE

The Ultimate Horror

Monday evening January 29, 1979, Bill got home from work, headed upstairs to Mrs. Gibson's apartment, and knocked on the door. Her daughter, Julie, answered the door and Bill asked her to watch the baby that night, explaining that Elaine wanted to do some housework and that he was going to the movies with his friends. Julie agreed and Bill went back downstairs.

Later in the evening Mrs. Gibson was in the Tyrees' apartment when Bill left to go to the movies. Mrs. Gibson recalls, "They had mentioned that it was payday. I don't know why it's called payday formation, and Elaine had to go, but Bill didn't have to go." She further states, "They had just finished dinner. They had dinner from the Trojan Room in downtown Ayer, and we discussed the leftover food and she said, 'I ate Bill's salad.' Bill then said he was going out and Elaine wanted to clean the apartment, and could Julie babysit? I said sure and then I left."

Sometime during the evening, Erik Aarhus knocked at the Tyrees' apartment door and Elaine invited him in. He said he was there to meet with Bill. She informed him that Bill was out but would be back if he cared to wait. Aarhus agreed and took a seat near the kitchen table. Julie Gibson came to the Tyrees' apartment around 8:00 p.m. to bring the baby back.

Elaine answered the door. She asked Julie to stay with her for a while because Aarhus was there, and she didn't feel comfortable around him. Elaine left the apartment to go to the laundry room. While she was gone, Julie and Aarhus remained in the apartment in awkward silence, not speaking a word to each other. When Elaine returned, Julie began a conversation.

Julie recalls, "Well, there were a lot of different conversations, but we talked about the box of candies that Bill had gotten Elaine, I think the night before. We talked about how nice and pretty it was. Elaine's army hat was lying on the table and I said to her, 'I can't believe you wear this hat. You know what you look like in it,' and stuff like that. Then we got to talking about the hat, and she said she always wanted to wear it like a helmet. And so, the man in the room (Aarhus) said, 'That's how a couple of friends and I used to wear it,' and he fixed it like that and then he fixed it back and put it on the baby's head.

"Also, I said to Elaine the other night when my mother and I came back from eating, Menzie and Bill were outside in the hall talking about something, and neither of them had a happy look on their faces. She said, 'Oh yeah, I remember that.' " Eventually, Eric Aarhus left and Bill arrived home around 10:30 in the evening.

Elaine informed Bill that she had told Aarhus she was going to the CID to turn in her diary when she mustered out of the army. Bill became infuriated with this.. He asked her to keep quiet about her plans for the diary. Elaine and Bill then headed to bed since they had to be up early to drop Dawn off at the babysitter's place in the morning.

Just as the alarm clock in Bill and Elaine's bedroom turned 12:35 a.m. on January 30, 1979, the telephone rang, startling the two of them from a sound sleep. Bill answered the phone and heard a warning from the other end: "Tell your wife to stop doing what she is doing or she is dead." Tyree immediately hung the phone up and proceeded to call his parents. When they answered, he informed them of the latest threat.

At 7:55 a.m., Elaine and Bill got into their pickup truck and Mrs. Gibson asked them for a ride. They dropped her off at the bus station downtown.

Mrs. Gibson recalls, "They were in the truck leaving to drive to work, and I was on my way out the door, and flagged them down for a ride. I asked her if she got up and went at 5:30, or whatever, and Elaine said yes, they had gone. I also asked Elaine to call Julie because when I walked out of the apartment, I was expecting to take my car to the bus station Then I realized it was getting very close to the time for the bus to leave, so I thought since they had the truck warm, you know, but Julie would be worried if she looked out later and found my car there. So, I asked Elaine to call Julie when she got to work and let her know that they had taken me to the bus station, and Elaine said she would."

Bill dropped Elaine off at work and headed for military traffic court. He had been cited for operating fog lights while on base. Afterwards, he went to see Aarhus. Bill recalls, "We spoke briefly. I told him to stay away from the apartment and that was it." He then went by the house and dropped off a baby carriage before heading back to the post to pick up Elaine. He didn't want to leave the baby carriage in the open bed in back of the truck because he feared someone might steal it All week long, they had been eating lunch together on post. On this particular day, Elaine informed Bill that she wouldn't be able to eat lunch with him because she had to go home and get her extra uniform so she could turn it in and out-process on time. Bill stopped at a local store so Elaine could get something to eat, then dropped her off and headed back to post to deliver to personnel in the

441st the typewriters he should have dealt with earlier had he not been in traffic court all morning.

Bill recalls, "It was a sunny, cold New England Tuesday at lunchtime. I dropped Elaine off at the apartment carrying her groceries we had stopped and bought on the way home. Her daily can of soup, a soda, that type of meal. She walked around our red four-wheel truck, and I opened the door. We kissed as we had a hundred times before that day. She smiled and walked away." Bill drove off and headed back to Fort Devens.

Mrs. Eliades, a resident of 104 ½ Washington Street and next-door neighbor of the Tyrees, heard a scream coming from the Tyree apartment at 12:00 noon. Mrs. Eliades states she heard, " 'Get out of here and leave me alone.' Then I heard a scream that you just could never believe. It was chilling." She immediately ran down the hall and began knocking frantically on the door. When she received no reply, she went back to her apartment and called the Ayer Police Department at 12:04 p.m.

Officer Walter Decott was dispatched to the scene and arrived at 12:07 p.m. Officer Decott knocked on the door at first and received no answer, so he knocked harder but to no avail. He checked the door and found it was locked.

Decott recalls, "She stated that there had been a lot of screaming coming from a female in Apartment 1 at that location. She led me to Apartment 1, which was through a little passageway down a small flight, possibly three or four steps, and the first apartment on the left-hand side. I banged on the door probably six or eight times, didn't receive any answer. I had a little stick here. I whacked the door very, very loud, and at that time announced, 'Police, police officer. Are you all, right?' While I was banging on the door attempting to get some response, there was a plastic mat on the floor in front of the door, clear plastic, and I looked down and observed six or eight round spots, which looked to me possibly to be blood drops on the floor and also on the door."

He then asked Mrs. Eliades who may have a master key to the apartment. She replied, "The landlord." Officer Decott and Mrs. Eliades walked outside toward the Ayer Police cruiser when they noticed the bedroom window screen on the ground outside of the Tyrees' bedroom window. The screen had not been there when Officer Decott entered the building.

Officer Decott further states, "I walked out of the building, down the stairs to the little porch area where I had just observed Mrs. Eliades, the reporting party, walked to my cruiser which was parked fifteen yards in the parking lot on the other side of the grassy area. I observed a screen on the right-hand side of the walkway and as I looked over toward the building, I observed the window, the lower portion of the window being open."

Chief William L. Adamson recalls, "On my arrival, the window from the bedroom entering onto the parking lot— there's a grassy plot around this part of the building—the window was open and lifted. There was a screen on the ground. The screen when I arrived was about six to seven feet from the window, right next to the blacktop walk that goes up to the door to the building. While waiting for the landlord to come, Officer Decott and myself, in fact, went to that window and we looked from the outside to see if we could see anything or anybody inside. We didn't see anything. There was under the window what appeared to be a scuff mark from a shoe or something. It was a definite impression in the vicinity of that window."

Approximately ten minutes after being called on the telephone the landlord, Mr. Francis Gardner, arrived to unlock the door to the apartment. Mr. Gardner owned a used car lot in town and was easily reachable. By this time, Ayer Police Chief William Adamson had arrived on scene and was waiting with Officer Decott. Once the door was opened, Adamson and Decott entered and found Elaine's lifeless body on the floor.

Chief Adamson states, "I secured the scene immediately when I walked in. Patrolman Decott was right behind me, never really got much past the threshold of the door, and as soon as I observed the subject on the floor, I initially requested an ambulance. After checking the person on the floor, I canceled the ambulance and I asked for the State Police and a medical examiner, and I permitted nobody else into the apartment until Trooper Hendrigan and Dr. Hopkins arrived."

Elaine was lying motionless on the floor, covered in blood and wearing her green army fatigues. Officer Decott recalls, "Chief Adamson asked me to get an ambulance right away. I had a portable radio with me at the time, and I didn't know whether it would transmit well from inside the building. I went out onto the porch area outside the building, called my station and asked them to send an ambulance, and told them to step on it. When I went back into the apartment after transmitting to my station, the chief said, 'Cancel the ambulance, ask for a medical examiner and contact the State Police detectives.' "

Adamson notified the district attorney's office to inform them of the homicide. They called Massachusetts State Police trooper Roderick Hendrigan to the scene at 104 ½ Washington Street. An hour and a half after Hendrigan's arrival, Massachusetts State Police detective Jack Dwyer arrived. Hendrigan searched the body and was able to retrieve Elaine's military identification card. The telephone in the apartment began to ring and Chief Adamson answered it. Bill was on the other end, demanding to speak with Elaine. Adamson informed him that an incident had occurred and they needed to speak with him at the apartment immediately. Bill agreed and left Fort Devens for downtown Ayer.

Chief Adamson recalls this moment. "It was 12:15. The telephone rang, and I was alone in the apartment. I answered the phone and it was a male subject on the other end. He asked who this was, and I asked who was calling. He stated that his name was William Tyree, and that he lived in the apartment where I was, and he wanted to know who I was, and what the problem was. I told him that I was a police officer, and I requested initially that he come to the apartment, that something had occurred. He asked me what had occurred, and I didn't want to say anything over the phone. I asked that he come to the apartment. The phone was suddenly hung up and in thinking about it, I felt as though it might be a better idea if he was directed to the police station, rather than walk into a scene such as I was in at that time. I placed a call to my cruiser to attempt to intercept him on the route from Fort Devens to Ayer."

Chief Adamson further states, "I felt at the time that whoever committed this murder had encountered the victim, Mrs. Tyree, in the hallway. The door leading to the cellar is adjacent, or directly across, or slightly behind the entrance to their apartment. I felt as though this person, or persons, may have secreted themselves on the stairway, where they could observe her coming in the hallway as she was opening the door, encountered her in the hallway and, whatever struggle ensued, went into the apartment. Based on the testing for blood that was found on the other door going down to the cellar, which was down the hall and to the rear of the building, I also felt there was a possibility that whoever committed it may have come back into the building and secreted himself in the cellar until they were able to leave."

Chief Adamson would later recant his initial hypothesis of how the crime occurred, even going as far as ignoring the blood spatter in the hallway and claiming the murderer was lying in wait in the apartment. However, this second hypothesis does not hold water due to the amount of blood found in the hallway.

Bertrand B. Hopkins, MD, was the medical examiner called from the Ayer Police Department at 12:31 p.m. on January 30, 1979. He arrived at 104 ½ Washington Street at approximately 12:45 p.m. and was met by Ayer Police Chief William Adamson.

Hopkins states in his official report, "I observed a woman dressed in army fatigues lying on her back on the floor of the apartment adjacent to the couch. I noted blood on her face and a large slash wound across the interior portion of her neck. In order not to disturb any necessary evidence, I did not carry on further examination but did indicate my decision to perform a complete autopsy as soon as it could be arranged. I then further viewed the apartment and discussed the situation and findings with Chief Adamson."

The autopsy was performed at the Nashoba Community Hospital at 4:45 p.m. The findings were follows:

1. Broad slash wound of throat with penetration of airway, left deep jugular vein and right common carotid artery and vagus nerve.

2. Superficial lacerations of chin.

3. Deep penetrating stab wound of neck.

4. Stab wound of left lateral neck.

5. Lacerations of left arm.

6. Stab wound of central anterior chest, with penetration of right and left lungs and pericardial sac; a massive hemorrhage.

7. Superficial stab wounds of left upper thorax.

8. Laceration of right finger.

9. Stab wounds of scalp.

Ambrose F. Keeley, MD, performed the autopsy and stated in his opinion that Elaine Tyree died of multiple stab wounds of the throat, chest, airway, jugular vein, and carotid artery: homicide.

Massachusetts State Police detective John Dwyer requested a chemist from the Massachusetts State crime lab to come to the apartment at 104 ½ Washington Street in Ayer. The chemist, Paul Conley, arrived at the crime scene to conduct benzidine reagent tests at the apartment. This test is used to detect the presence of human blood that may have been wiped up.

His visual observations revealed the following:

1. No blood in the kitchen sink.

2. Traces of blood in the bathroom sink and on the faucet knobs.

3. No blood in the shower area.

4. No blood on the sill or frame of the open bedroom window.

5. No blood on any of the extraneous garments in the apartment.

6. Numerous blood drippings on the lower half of the outside (hallway) surface of the door at the entrance to the apartment.

7. An array of fine blood splatters fanning out toward the front room from the victim's head and covering the area of the overturned sofa (and laundry) and having a radius of approximately 3 feet.

8. A heavy black smudge having the appearance of a boot scuff mark on the hallway wall of the living

room approximately 3 ½ feet above the floor and 5 feet left of the door to the apartment.

9. A broken lamp table (leg split off literally) overturned lamp, and scattered playing cards (bloodstained) in the area directly in front of the above-described scuff mark.

10. Numerous blood droplets on the carpet in the area of the overturned table described above.

These findings show a struggle between Elaine Tyree and her assailant or assailants. The scuff mark on the wall came from the murderer because Elaine's boots were not scuffed. Elaine definitely fought back against her murderer. It is also important to realize that Elaine had some self-defense training during her time in the military. She was not a mousey female but rather, someone who could handle herself. Therefore, her assailant had to have been between six foot and six foot two. A smaller, five foot, five inch man couldn't have produced those wounds on her.

CID agent Paul Mason remembers that day. While at the CID Headquarters they received word that the murder of a soldier had taken place. He states, "Joe (Burzynski) and I jumped in the car and we drove to that location in Ayer and it was frantic. We originally didn't get into the crime scene or get involved with the police. The off-post liaison folks were there, I think there was a staff sergeant working with them and the State seemed happy with it. Joe knew her and knew Bill Tyree, so he wanted to go and see where we could help about what's going on. But we didn't get involved right away. We got up to that house and started getting bits of info, you know? Joe looked at me and I looked at him and he just went, 'Tyree,' and I know there's something wrong, something stinks here. There was no request to us, if you will. It wasn't till later; it was a day or two later that the State Police, along with the sergeant from AWOL Apprehension came in and wanted our help and what we could do to help them. And then later, we got to see the crime scene and we walked through it."

It is fascinating that the CID was not requested by any police agency to show up and assist at the crime scene. Yet when the CID office heard about the murder of a soldier and post personnel that were requested by authorities and were already on scene, that the CID agent who was the investigator in Tyree's Article 15 made it a point to attempt to involve himself in the investigation under the guise of assisting. However, no other CID agent on duty that day saw the need to go and offer assistance. This gesture by Burzynski has the appearance of an agent who was eager to get a second shot at potentially prosecuting Tyree. His actions make him seem anything but impartial.

Officer Decott was dispatched from the crime scene and told to intercept Bill and escort him to the Ayer Police station. Officer Decott pulled Bill over about one eighth of a mile from the main gate at Fort Devens and had him lock up his truck and get into the cruiser for the ride to the station.

As Bill entered the station, he was greeted by Ayer Police lieutenant Arthur Boisseau, who had just returned from the crime scene. He read Bill his Miranda rights and had him sign a card acknowledging the fact. He proceeded to ask Bill what time he had dropped off his wife. Tyree replied that he had done so at 12:04 p.m., but he didn't go into the apartment and had returned to Fort Devens. When asked what time he had arrived on post, he replied 12:15 p.m. He informed them that he had spoken to Captain Klein, who asked him for the time. Boisseau then informed Bill of his wife's death.

Arthur Boisseau recalls, "Well, I received a radio call. I was returning from Boston. I was on route to, approximately in the area of Acton, when I received a radio call asking me to come to the station as fast as I could. Once I got into the center of town, I received a second communication to go to 104 ½ Washington Street, pick up my camera *en route* for whatever photos might have to be taken. When I arrived there, I was met just inside the main door to the building by Chief Adamson. There was a trooper Roderick Hendrigan with the chief. At this time, the chief took me into the room and stated, 'We've got a body here, so be very careful as to preserve the scene.' And he led me through the area while I took several pictures of the scene. I then left the scene, returned to the police station at the direction of the chief, and I had a conversation with Mr. Tyree. I advised him of his rights by the Miranda warning card. At that time, I advised him, by using the card, of his rights, that I was a police officer. I identified myself to him with my identification card, as I was in civilian clothes. I told him that he had the right to remain silent. I read right from the card. He agreed to talk to me under this Miranda. He said he understood his rights and that he would talk with me. I then presented him with the card to read and sign in the space provided. I advised Mr. Tyree that I had been sent to the station to advise him of an unfortunate situation. Then I told him that his wife was deceased at the apartment at 104 ½ Washington Street. Well, at this time, the room became silent, a word wasn't spoken for I'd say what seemed like a couple of minutes.

"Then Mr. Tyree put his hands to his face, got up from the chair, and walked around the room. When he came in front of me, I believe he sat down again. At this time, he asked me if I was sure it was his wife. I told him I was advised that it was Mrs. Tyree and it was his wife. I did not know the woman and did not identify her at the time I was at the apartment."

Since Boisseau also took photos of the crime scene he stated, "There appeared to be some stains on the outside of the apartment door and the room was in a state of upheaval. There was a sofa that was turned or appeared might have been broken. It was open, the bedroom window was open. I believe a lamp was tipped off a table in that bedroom."

Almost instantly, everyone wanted to know what Tyree had been doing during the day of the murder. Everyone he had any contact with at all was questioned. Bruce Beecham recalls, "At approximately 10:30 a.m., we were unloading... No, Tyree unloaded some typewriters from his truck and put them on the loading dock. I happened to be coming up just at that time. I said hello, and the usual, how are you, and like that, and we started talking about something, which I don't really remember what it was, but halfway through the conversation, he sort of looked over my shoulder across the field behind me and smiled and waved. I looked back across my shoulder to my left, and asked who he was waving at. He stated that it was his wife, that she worked across on the other side of the field. I then said, 'Oh, okay,' and he carried two typewriters in and I carried one in for him to give him a hand."

Another man who was questioned intensely was First Lieutenant John Klein III, the purchasing agent at the Director of Industrial Operations. Originally, First Lieutenant Klein was assigned to the 441st Military Detachment. On the morning of January 30, 1979, Klein saw Tyree several times throughout that day. He recalls, "I saw him earlier in the day. He was downstairs in what I call the headquarters section area. He was working on a typewriter problem. I left early for lunch, around 11:30, and failed to sign out on a sign outboard which tells where you are going and how long you'll be at a specific place. So therefore, I was rather conscious of the time, and I left my place according to my clock in the room at the Bachelor Officers Quarters Fort Devens at approximately three minutes past twelve. It takes about five minutes to get back to the unit, et cetera, so I figure it was about eight or nine past twelve when I arrived, and I sat at my desk for about five minutes when I decided I would check and see who had come back to the unit. I was going to the rear of the building to find out whose car was in the back.

"At that time, Tyree came into the building; entered the detachment. He asked what time it was, his watch was not working, and that he wanted to keep up the board accurately. I told him I didn't wear jewelry or a watch, and I didn't know for sure. But I thought it had to be a little bit past twelve, and he said, 'Does 12:15 sound all right?' He left, and I went back to my desk after that, and then he mentioned that he had been involved in a court case involving a traffic violation, and mentioned that if the MP failed to attend the court hearing, or whatever it was at that time. Again, apparently the MP had been late several times, then the judge was going to throw it out if the MP didn't have the gumption to come to the trial next time."

Bill Tyree went over and over the same sequence of events for the day in the conference room with Officer Boisseau. He even gave his permission for his truck to be searched and handed over his clothing for chemical analysis. No trace of blood was found on his clothing and no evidentiary evidence was found in the truck. It is important to note that neither the Ayer Police Department nor the Massachusetts State Police ever made an attempt to get authorization from Tyree or the court to obtain a search warrant for the apartment. It is hard to believe that something as important as a search warrant could have been overlooked by two police departments. After finding Elaine's body they searched the apartment, which begs the question: what were they looking for from the outset that they couldn't or wouldn't wait for a search warrant? Later in the evening, Tyree was taken to his apartment to get a few things for himself and the baby, who was staying with the sitter. He was then dropped off at the post and placed under guard.

Dennis Testagrossa, a soldier in Service Company 10th SFG (A) was charged with following Bill around the post and keeping tabs on him. When Earl Michael Peters returned from a four-day pass, he was ordered to follow Bill around and Testagrossa was relieved of the duty.

Also that evening, Massachusetts State trooper John Dwyer telephoned Massachusetts State trooper Patrick Keane to inform him of the homicide and request his assistance with the investigation. Keane agreed to the request and the two men briefly discussed the gruesome details of the case, then agreed to meet up the next morning.

On the morning of Wednesday, January 31, 1979, Keene, Dwyer, and Adamson went to the apartment, where they stayed for approximately thirty minutes. They walked through the scene, going over different scenarios and searching the premises.

Tyree was again interviewed by police officers in a conference room at the Criminal Investigation Division building at Fort Devens. The building was a converted World War II T barracks. This two-story wooden structure housed offices, interrogation rooms, holding cells, and a conference room.

At Tyree's request, he was taken to see Elaine's body at the local funeral home. While officers were in the room, he pulled the sheet covering her body down to her knees, kissed her forehead, and inspected her wounds. He tried to maintain his composure, but it was to no avail. His eyes filled with tears at the sight of his wife's body. When finally he was able to speak, he requested the funeral director turn Elaine's body over, as the police had informed Tyree that one of the stab wounds went through Elaine's body. After looking at the wounds on her back, Tyree told police there was only one kind of knife that was long enough and wide enough to have made the wounds. It was the kind of knife riggers use and he would find out who did it and take care of it his own way. Tyree was then returned to Fort Devens and again placed under guard.

Tyree recalls, "Chief Adamson, some other Massachusetts State patrol officers and I went to the morgue so that I could view the body and make sure it was Elaine. I started crying bad when I saw all the stitches. The police told me what type of knife they were looking for and based on that I described in detail what type of knife was used, because Peters told me Aarhus carried a Buck Pathfinder and I knew right then and there I had to get who did it."

Later that evening, Keane, Hendrigan, Dwyer, and Adamson accompanied Bill to the house so he could get one of Elaine's dresses for the funeral home. Hendrigan asked if he could accompany him inside and Tyree agreed. They looked around the home for thirty minutes. Hendrigan took a New York traffic ticket he found on the table in the apartment.

Police investigators also went door to door to the surrounding apartments to see if anyone might have witnessed anything. Vias Williams, a soldier who lived in the apartment building across the parking lot from the Tyrees, informed investigators that around the time of the murder he saw a man running alongside his building.

"Hard pressed on my right. My center is yielding. Impossible to maneuver. Situation excellent. I am attacking." Ferdinand Foch at the Battle of the Marne

CHAPTER FOUR

The Knock on the Door

The next day, the CID began investigating several soldiers at Fort Devens. One soldier they interviewed was Erik Aarhus, who was interviewed in the evening at CID headquarters. He was initially ruled out as a suspect due to the cast on his leg from mid-thigh to mid-calf. US Army medical records verified that Aarhus had suffered an injury to his leg prior to the murder. He was not physically capable of running from the crime scene as one witness stated they had seen a man run from the scene.

The CID initially thought that a man with a cast on his leg wouldn't be able to jump out a window and run from a murder scene. The CID asked Aarhus for permission to search his barracks room. He gave permission to search and the CID and the Massachusetts State Police thoroughly searched the room and the wall locker as well. No bloody clothing or weapon or anything that connected Aarhus to the murder could be found. It appeared to the investigators that Erik Aarhus seemed to be under some kind of narcotic during the interview. It is important to note that this first room search was never authorized or documented with post commander Colonel Rittgers.

Bill later states, "I played around with Chief Adamson and never did even to this day level with him. I couldn't because even up until the day I was arrested I didn't know who did it. I was really just feeding the chief a line, because he kept asking me if Rosario could be involved. He wanted Rosario with a passion as did the State Police because of his alleged drug dealing, gun running, and drug smuggling. They thought a murder like this had to be involved with dope. Rosario was in the same company and I knew him so the police kept asking about him." At a point in time prior to February 13, 1979, the Ayer Police verified Rosario's whereabouts. He had an airtight alibi for the time of the murder: he was handcuffed to a Massachusetts State trooper in a courthouse at the time Elaine was killed.

On Thursday, February 1, 1979, soldier Dennis Testagrossa was the guard placed on Tyree. Testagrossa was good friends and roommate to Earl Michael Peters. Tyree was unjustly placed under guard and deprived of his freedom of coming and going at will. All his activities were closely monitored by the guards assigned to him and while under guard, he was never allowed to consult with a lawyer. Furthermore, it is questionable as to why Testagrossa was assigned since he ran with the same crowd as Tyree and all were under CID suspicion. To be placed under guard by the army is usually done because you are either under arrest—which Tyree was not—or you are under suicide watch, which clearly was not the case since Tyree was never sent to Mental Health for an evaluation or made claims of suicidal ideation. It would have made more sense to place an MP or another impartial soldier as a guard.

While watching Tyree, Testagrossa allegedly overheard, and testified to, a conversation between Tyree an unidentified sergeant and another person during which Tyree described in graphic detail how he envisioned the murder of his wife.

CID was also conducting a covert investigation with the help of Vias Williams. He recalls, "After the night they initially talked to me, they came to my work several times and took me from my workplace and we went and did some stakeouts, generally around Special Forces Group, and the places they worked around to see if I recognized anybody that fit the description of the person I saw run that day. And they also took me to two or three lineups where they marched people in on a stage and had them face left to see if I could recognize anybody there, and I never did. They also tried to hypnotize me two or three times to see if they could jog my memory a little bit more about what his face looked like, to help the lineups and the stakeouts we had gone out on." What is interesting about the CID investigation that Mr. Williams was a part of is why he was not shown mug-shots at the Ayer or State Police station to see if the event could have possibly involved a civilian. The CID investigation, along with Ayer Police and the State Police, concentrated solely on military personnel.

Also, it is unknown if Earl Michael Peters was ever involved in any of these lineups or if he was present during these stakeouts.

***

Trooper Keane returned to the apartment with Chief Adamson and Detective Dwyer. They continued searching and took two letters they found in a coffee can in a cabinet above the refrigerator. They stayed for over an hour in the apartment. The Ayer Police retained a key to the apartment until February 21, 1979. No search warrant was ever obtained, even though there were other police visits to the apartment during that time. Elaine's diaries were never found in the apartment. It is widely believed that Dwyer found Elaine's diaries and handed them over to Colonel Cutolo rather than use them as evidence for the trial.

On Saturday, February 3, 1979, a party of service people from Fort Devens arrived in Cumberland, Maryland. The party consisted of pall bearers and an honor guard.

Staff Sergeant Robert Mitchell Jr. recalls, "I was a counterintelligence special agent for Military Intelligence. I'm not really sure who it was that chose me. I was told by First Sergeant Henry that I had been chosen to go down there. We arrived on Saturday morning in Cumberland, Maryland; we stayed at the Holiday Inn. I had a chance to see Tyree that evening in a restaurant at the hotel. I was standing there. There were a couple of other people that were with the party that were talking to him at that time. I don't recall everything in the conversation. Basically, it was, you know, the general how's everything going? On Sunday morning, Master Sgt. Matthews and I went to the funeral home to make prior arrangements and everything. We were the pallbearers, so we would be at the funeral home, and Tyree was there at the same time. He was going around making sure everything was set up right and everything at the funeral home for the proceedings that afternoon. He was conversing with the funeral director and everything, trying to make sure that everything had been taken care of and all the arrangements were made."

The next day, Elaine was buried. Sally Fisher, a clerk in the ID section of Fort Devens and a member of the funeral detachment, was at the bereavement party. She recalls the events, "We were sitting at a table. They offered us something to eat. Well, we were all sitting around the table real quiet, and the first thing that he (Bill) said when he walked in was, 'What happened, you guys look like somebody just died.' We all sort of just looked at each other like we didn't know what to say."

Many of the people in attendance at the wake and funeral thought it strange that Bill had chosen certain songs such as "Tuesday Afternoon" by the Moody Blues. Bill recalls, "I chose the songs that Elaine liked to hear the most, whenever we would be in the truck going somewhere. She also liked

'Bat out of Hell' by Meatloaf, but I decided against that song."

Mitchell Jr. further recalls the events after the funeral. "It was about 10:30 that night, in a bar there at the Holiday Inn. I observed Tyree at the table with some of the members of the firing party, funeral detail, at a table in the bar where we were at. They were laughing and talking and having a few drinks."

First Sergeant Henry was also present at the funeral as part of the military detail sent from Fort Devens. He recalls, "There were some hard feelings between my people and Tyree. I sort of told him that, you know, we wanted to be left alone. We'll go our way. We did our detail, and we just want to get back. He just wanted to pay for our drinks, and the waitress was a little perturbed about it. Sgt. Neikov and Sgt. Mitchell definitely wanted a piece of Private Tyree."

"This was all due to the media," Bill recalls. "Articles had my daughter crawling around in my wife's blood. My daughter was sixty-seven days old; she couldn't do anything but sleep and eat. As for Neikov, he was a Russian Army defector who would side with the majority in order to fit it. Mitchell was the unofficial enforcer for the detachment and the go to guy for First Sgt. Henry. We never got along, especially after the 441st Detachment party at Captain Williams' home on post, where he had to be told by First Sgt. Henry to give Elaine some distance because Mitchell was all over her. Elaine told me about it later. As soon as Mitchell heard that CID was interested in me, he was in aggressive mode."

Bill was a man without a country. Everyone within his unit and some of the adjoining units knew or had heard rumors about his Article 15. They figured he was not an honorable person or soldier. The damage to his reputation had been done, and now he was a casualty in the aftermath of Elaine's death. Soldiers who had once befriended him now viewed him with an eye of suspicion, figuring that if he stole from the army as he had initially been charged, he could have had a hand in his wife's murder. It was also during this time that Elaine's parents stepped in to take care of Dawn, since Bill was in no state of mind to care for a baby.

Another anomaly concerning Elaine's funeral centers on the personnel who were sent to Maryland as the honor guard. Elaine was not Airborne, Military Intelligence, or Special Forces. She was simply a clerk in the regular army, so why send these people? This was extremely unusual and the fact that they sent Mitchell, with whom Bill had problems, was even stranger. It has been speculated that they were sent to possibly keep an eye on Bill. Again, however, this is just speculation.

At approximately 2:30 a.m., Dennis Testagrossa allegedly received a phone call from Tyree, who was still in Maryland. Tyree requested that he call a telephone number and say that Aarhus did it. The MP office at Fort Devens received a telephone call from an unidentified man who spelled Aarhus's name phonetically and stated that he killed Elaine Tyree. The desk sergeant relayed the message to the Ayer Police Department. It is important to note that no phone records could be found by the Massachusetts State Police, the CID, or the FBI to confirm that the call originated from Bill Tyree.

This mysterious phone call has long been at the center of a lot of controversy, the reason being that Aarhus had been cleared as a suspect four days earlier. However, someone was still trying to keep him under suspicion. Once Aarhus was cleared, only law enforcement could bring the investigation back to him. This is one of the major anomalies in this case. Bill has always vehemently denied making the call and the phone records prove he didn't, so the big question is, who did and why?

Several witnesses saw Bill drinking doubles in the hotel bar that night after his wife's funeral. Michael Arena, who was a member of the funeral party from Fort Devens, states, "I got a call in my room from Bill. He was a little bit incoherent, but he said somebody had hit him in the head, and I asked him where he was. He said he was up in his room. It was around 11:30. So, I and Michelle Lafax went upstairs to his room."

Michelle Lafax remembers, "Tyree stated that somebody was trying to get him, and that he wanted help. So, we went upstairs because we could hear as if the windows were open and the wind was blowing in the room. We thought he was going to jump, so we went upstairs. The door was open and that's when we found him in the bathtub in a t-shirt."

Arena added under oath, "When I came to the door it was ajar, and I walked in. I called out his name and he answered from the bathroom. He was in the bathtub with the shower curtain drawn. I helped him out of the tub and suggested he go to bed, since there weren't any cuts on his head or bruises. I went back to my room and then twenty minutes had passed. There was a knock at the door and Captain Cote was there with William Tyree's father, and he said that Bill Tyree had been taken to the hospital and he wasn't sure of the circumstances of what had happened and would I take his father to the hospital? So, I got Bob McQuire and took Mr. Tyree Sr. to the hospital.

"Upon our arrival, we were met just inside the emergency room by police officers who told us that they had received a call from the hotel, that Bill Tyree had called down to the desk and that he had been assaulted, hit in the head. The police responded, they went up to the room, and the officer told us that the door was locked and they had to kick the door down. At this point, a police lieutenant approached the officer and asked what he was still doing there. The officer explained the call and that Bill Tyree was starting to act up, wasn't being cooperative, arrogant, and felt he should stay. He said that as far as he knew, Bill Tyree had a black belt in karate and that Tyree was a good-sized guy. At that point, the lieutenant said that these two soldiers are here, referring to McQuire and myself. He said to let us handle it; it's the army's problem now. So, we went.

"A nurse took us into a treatment room. Bill was sitting at the edge of the stretcher, and there were two nurses and a doctor there with him. The doctor called me out of the room and asked if I knew what the situation was and Bill Tyree, I can't recall exactly what he wanted to do, and they wanted him to stay on the stretcher. He pushed the two orderlies back, and he got what I surmised a karate stance.

"So, at that point myself and Bob McQuire, the two orderlies, and the doctor rushed him. McQuire and I grabbed his arms. The two orderlies grabbed his legs, and we pulled him back on the stretcher. He started screaming really loud. His father came into the room, and we were holding him down. The doctor told the nurse to get some Thorazine. So, we were holding him down, and his father was there, and he started screaming at his father. He was saying, 'You're no fucking good, Dad. I'll kill you. Get out of my sight. I never want to see you again!' He was saying that and repeated it a couple of times. McQuire and I kept holding him down and he kept repeating he knew who did it. He kept screaming, and then he said, 'Do you know who did it?' He goes, 'I did it, but I'm not telling you who did it.' It just didn't make any sense to me. Then he started screaming at McQuire and I. "Why are you doing this to me? We tried to explain that we were just holding him down, and then he said, 'You're dead.' He said, 'You're both dead, your wives are dead.' He said the funeral detail is dead. Then he changed again, and he started screaming for Captain Carrigan. He wanted to see him. We said he couldn't see Carrigan. He said that he had to talk to him. He had to talk to him immediately or somebody is going to be dead.

"The nurse came in prior to this and had given him a shot. I asked what she gave him, and she said a hundred milligrams of Thorazine. The drug started to take effect and he finally fell asleep, became unconscious. At that point, I went with his father and the doctor into the office because they had tied him down. They had secured him down. I helped his father; his father was quite upset and was having some trouble trying to find identification of Bill's to be able to fill out the medical chart. The doctor remarked to me that he was sending him to a local psychiatric hospital, that he didn't feel Bill was capable of doing exactly what he said, and he wanted to send him to a psychiatric unit for observation.

"An ambulance came and took Bill Tyree and his father to a local psychiatric unit. His father was with him. We had called Captain Cote prior to the ambulance coming, and he wanted us as soon as Tyree was transported to come back and give him a full report of what had happened."

Bill was held in the primary US Army Hospital at Walter Reed for observation for a week until being released on February 9, 1979, and returned to Fort Devens. This was the first and only time that Tyree exhibited signs of a mental breakdown. While at Walter Reed, his medical file noted that he had been admitted for acute alcohol intoxication manifested by headache, confusion, and stress. The clinical record goes on to say that Bill had been suffering from depression, loss of sleep and appetite, and ten pounds of weight loss. The record states, "Patient has had homicidal thoughts when his wife was first killed. Patient states he has killed a man before. Patient appears to be dealing well.

Patient needs some rest and maybe a new duty station, maybe closer to home."

Arena further recalls, "About a week later, he came into the orderly room. There was another soldier with him. He was the same soldier who was with him just before we departed to Maryland, when he came in to see Captain Cote about the arrangements. All he said to me was, 'They said I'm all right to be out at Walter Reed.' I just remarked that's good."

Later in the day, Bill met with Chief Adamson at the Ayer Police station. Adamson asked if he was willing to take a polygraph and Bill agreed. However, he had one condition, that being that they only ask him one question: Did I kill her? Tyree was then taken back to Fort Devens and sent to Earl Michael Peters' room to be guarded. This time, a guard was warranted since he had just been released from Walter Reed for a mental breakdown. However, again the guard was Peters, with whom he had been under suspicion earlier by the CID. Bill said he recalled nothing of the breakdown, except, "What my dad had told me that I said I know who did it, I know who did it. I should have been there."

Chief Adamson recalls a meeting with Tyree. "I believe the next time was on the 9th of February, in the evening. He came to the Ayer Police station, accompanied by a military police investigator, Mr. Burke." Chief Adamson testified that this case also involved another soldier who was allegedly in possession of $2 million in heroin that he kept in a military type footlocker in the back of his vehicle. This only surfaced during the course of the Elaine Tyree murder investigation.

Adamson further states, "On the 30th of November, 1978, or December 1, 1978, he had not received his paycheck. He had gone to the Service Company 10th SFG at about 10:00 in the morning with his wife to see if his check was at the company. He alleges that this other soldier came walking in from the barracks area of one of the buildings, carrying a garment-type bag. The bag appeared to contain something besides clothes and was difficult to handle; or at least seemed so. He alleges that the soldier started to stuff this bag into his vehicle, the same yellow car. Then an M-16 weapon fell out onto the ground. Mr. Tyree said to him at that time, 'That's outstanding, where did you get it?' The soldier was alleged to have replied, 'I've got three of them.'

"Bill told the other soldier he didn't wish to get involved and he went inside to claim his check, and come back out. They departed. Mrs. Tyree, Elaine Tyree, was in the truck and also saw this weapon fall onto the ground."

Bill recalls, "About the third week of December, 1978, while we were at Service Company picking up my mail, Aarhus approached Elaine. She and the baby were in the truck, and Aarhus asked her about the books. She told him she had the books, but she had gotten rid of them. He told her for her sake she had better. Later on, when I asked him who told him about the books, he said Earl Michael Peters. I then asked him why he wanted the books. He said, 'Because with those books I could go to jail.' Peters was at my house the Saturday night before Elaine died. Peters, Elaine, and I discussed what we would do with the books. At that point, Peters discovered his name was in the books as often as Aarhus. He got mad and asked me to drive him back to post. On the ride back, he told me that with books like those floating around, 'Someone could get their throat cut.' " This statement was later corroborated by Sgt. Menzie during the probable cause hearing before Judge Killam.

Bill maintains that just before Christmas 1978, he went to Service Company and when he came out, he found a handwritten note in black marker, which said, "Keep your mouth shut, and nothing will happen." I asked him where the note was, and his reply was, "I deep-sixed it because it didn't bother me. I told my father about the first one."

Chief Adamson continues, "About two days later, another note written on yellow massage paper, which Mr. Tyree states is a standard army form, was found stuck under the windshield wiper of his truck. He stated that the message was basically the same.

"Approximately three days after that, his wife was seated in the truck, waiting for him outside the company, and someone apparently dropped a note on the ground in the vicinity of the truck. What was the interval between the first note and the second? He stated that a fourth note was found taped to their apartment door about the middle of December 1978. This note was in red ink and stated that Elaine had called her parents about it and advised them. He said that no more notes were received.

"About the second week of January 1979 on a Sunday, the phone rang. His wife took the phone and handed it to him. A male voice said, 'You might have won over this turn, but you'll get yours in the future.' We questioned Mr. Tyree. 'Did you recognize the voice?' He said he was unsure; it possibly sounded like another soldier. He stated he got angry and he threw the phone. He told me that they had received about six more calls. He took three and his wife, Elaine, took three and basically, the caller stated the same thing each time.

"The last call was received after midnight on January 30, 1979, and Mr. Tyree stated he was asleep and didn't hear the phone ring. He stated that something woke him up. He was at a loss to explain what it was. His wife, Elaine, had the phone in her hand. She started crying and she just threw the phone across the room and everything on the table next to the bed came off. He asked her what was said and she wouldn't tell him. He said they were both shook up and the baby started fussing and they didn't sleep much, or at all the rest of the night.

"I then questioned him about what happened in Maryland and he replied, 'I don't know. I started drinking at the hotel after the funeral. I was drinking everything, including tequila. I went to my room and all I remember is when I opened the door to my room, I saw a shadow in the room. Next thing I remember, I was in a hospital in a straitjacket, and they told me I had flipped out.' He told me, 'You can check this with the manager of the Holiday Inn in Cumberland, Maryland. I called and asked them to send someone to my room.' I asked him if he called any of his buddies at the hotel and that they come to his room. He replied, 'No. I called the desk and I asked that somebody be sent up.' He stated that his sister was grabbed on an Amtrak, sometime in February 1979, on her way home from Elaine's funeral by an unknown subject who allegedly stuck a knife to her throat and said, 'Tell everyone to keep their mouth shut and nothing will happen.' She couldn't identify the subject. The remainder of the conversation was relative to when he could take a leave to get his head straight and arrange for a discharge from the army. The interview concluded after that."

***

The next day, Peters asked Tyree what he thought had happened to his wife. Tyree said he thought Aarhus had killed her.

On Monday, February 12, 1979, Tyree was again questioned by the Ayer Police Department. When confronted about several inconsistencies, he admitted he had met Aarhus sometime between 11:00 a.m. and noon on the day Elaine was killed. Tyree had asked Aarhus what he had been doing at Tyree's apartment Monday evening the day before the murder. Aarhus explained that he had been visiting a friend in the building next door. After the interview was concluded, Tyree returned to the post.

Meanwhile, the CID was still questioning post personnel and trying to find out who was responsible for the murder. One of the men they interviewed was Kenneth, a truck driver and roommate of Dennis Testagrossa and Earl Michael Peters.

PFC Yow recalled that on the day of the murder, Peters had CQ duty. This duty required him to stay at a spot for twenty-four hours after duty hours. He stated, "One person is assigned to stay there from 4:30 to 7:00 the morning until he is relieved. When I broke for lunch, I came back, and he (Peters) was in the room in bed. I stayed in the room for fifteen minutes and then I went to chow. He woke up while I was in the room. When I returned to the room after chow, Testagrossa, Peters, and PFC Guertin were all in the room."

This was enough evidence for the CID to not look at Peters any further for the murder of Elaine Tyree. While on CQ, Peters could have left his post to go to the bathroom or sick bay. He was also given an hour for chow. The Massachusetts State Police testified that it only took eleven minutes to drive from Peters' barracks room in Service Company to the Tyree apartment. Yet the CID agents never looked further.

On February 12, 1979, Erik Aarhus and several other suspects met at the CID headquarters. CID agent Burzynski marched these men to an athletic field a short distance from the CID building. He had them line up and asked the men to run approximately fifty yards. Aarhus was unable to perform the task due to a previous injury where he hurt his back and pulled ligaments, requiring him to wear a cast on his leg. Aarhus's injury occurred prior to Elaine's murder. Fellow soldier and neighbor of Bill and Elaine, Vias Williams, who witnessed a man running on ice and snow near the woods beside the apartment at the time of the murder, watched these men run.

***

On February 13, 1979, everything changed. At 7:30 a.m., Tyree was eating in the 39th Engineers mess hall when he was approached by Earl Michael Peters, who sat down and proceeded to talk to him about the death of his wife. Peters stated that whoever had killed her and whatever they had used must have been wrapped in plastic. He then implicated Aarhus as Elaine's murderer. As Bill dwelled on what Peters said, he concocted a plan. Before noon, Bill called his friend, Mike Menzie, and relayed the information that Peters had divulged to him.

He approached Aarhus in his room at 12:30 p.m. at the Service Company. He informed Aarhus that he had done him a favor by killing his wife and offered him money for the murder weapon. Aarhus agreed to get the knife and was delighted at the thought of making some money for his time, and plans were made.

Bill's whereabouts were not documented for a period of time until he called Range Control before 1:00 p.m. Then Sgt. Menzie called Chief Adamson and informed him of his new discovery about the alleged murder weapon.

Chief Adamson formed a plan whereas Bill would receive the knife from Aarhus in the parking lot of Devens Shopping Center, a strip mall just outside of Verbeck Gate at Fort Devens. Bill would wait in his truck and once Aarhus approached and handed him the alleged murder weapon, he would turn his windshield wipers on to alert the nearby police to move in and arrest Aarhus. This plan was devised because Chief Adamson couldn't come on Fort Devens property and seize any evidence as he had no jurisdiction on federal property. Then Aarhus backed out because he was on restricted duty and couldn't leave the post.

Bill further states, "I didn't call Adamson about Aarhus having the alleged murder weapon. I spoke to Adamson about Aarhus being the fall guy, and I felt Aarhus was just the guy left holding the knife. Sgt. Menzie told me after I spoke to Adamson that he (Adamson) was on his way to the Fort Devens CID office.

Sgt. Menzie then called Chief Adamson, who informed him that he was on his way to the Fort Devens CID office, along with Massachusetts State Police officers Dwyer and Keane, and Ayer Police officer Lisanao. They all arrived at the CID headquarters at 5:30 p.m. Sgt. Menzie left at the same time to pick up his girlfriend from work. Aarhus left the riggers shed at Moore Army Airfield at 5:00 p.m. and arrived at Service Company barracks, where he parked the truck. He was in his room at 5:15 p.m.

Shortly after Aarhus entered his room, Bill knocked at the door. He asked Aarhus for the knife and was informed that he didn't have it but was still willing to retrieve it. Bill says this was when he knew that Aarhus was the fall guy and not the killer. Aarhus headed out of his room to go pull some extra duty he had been assigned in the barracks, and Bill headed upstairs to Peters' room. Bill found both Peters and Testagrossa in the room and informed Peters that Aarhus still had not got the knife. Peters informed him that he had just been in Aarhus's room and seen him take the knife out of his coat and place it under his pillow. Bill states that at this exact moment, he was sure that Peters was Elaine's killer.

According to Bill, Dennis Testagrossa was not a party to the conversation. Bill left Peters and headed downstairs to wait for Menzie and his girlfriend to come by. While Bill was waiting, Peters approached him in front of the dayroom windows in Service Company and pulled a .45 caliber handgun out of his army parka, pointed it at Bill, and proceeded to tell him what had happened on the afternoon when Elaine was murdered. He told Bill he didn't want to kill her, but he had no choice as she had diaries with stuff on all of them. Bill was not in complete shock as Peters talked. He had been putting the pieces together since the murder. All Peters did was confirm most of it and fill in a few missing pieces. Just then, several cars approached the barracks as Peters headed back inside. Menzie and his girlfriend, Nancy Woodland, were in the first car. They pulled up and told Bill to get in. Bill got in the car and as they were pulling out of the barracks parking lot, the other cars were pulling in. The other automobiles were from the CID and the Ayer Police Department.

Menzie drove Bill to the CID and he entered the building at 5:55 p.m. Bill states that he had no intention of going to the CID, nor did he really want to, due to his distrust of the CID during the prior year's events As Bill was entering the CID and waiting to speak to CID agent Burzynski, the CID was already on scene searching Aarhus's room in the Service Company barracks by 6:00 p.m. Special Agent Mason testified that at 6:15 p.m., he seized the alleged murder weapon, a knife with dried blood on it taken from beneath Erik Aarhus's pillow.

When Bill was finally met by CID agent Joseph Burzynski, he was taken to a room and asked to write a statement about who, how, and when he was told about the knife. According to Bill, each time he began the statement and mentioned Earl Michael Peters informing him the knife being wrapped in plastic, Agent Burzynski would tear up the statement and say no, it was Aarhus who told you. After this happened several times, Bill finally wrote a statement that is time stamped at 6:33 p.m. He lied in this statement because Agent Burzynski was threatening him with arrest, so he wrote what Burzynski told him to write. This statement names Aarhus as the person at breakfast who informed him of the knife being wrapped in a plastic bag, instead of Peters.

Chief Adamson recalls the events of the day, stating, "On the 13th of February, approximately 2:00 in the afternoon, I was called by another party, Sgt. Menzie, on his (Bill's) behalf. He stated, 'Hey you had been talking to Tyree and Tyree had approached Aarhus that day. He told Aarhus that he wanted the knife. He told him that he had arranged for a relative to pick up the knife that day, and he was going to carry the knife out of state.' He stated that he 'knew Aarhus had the knife, that he didn't care, that he just wanted to get the knife out of state so he couldn't be connected with it,' and he had offered Aarhus a sum of money to recover this knife and deliver it to him.

"I asked Sgt. Menzie where Mr. Tyree was and he said, 'He's right here.' I said, 'Well, put him on the phone so I can talk to him.' Mr. Tyree came onto the phone and he told me that he had seen Aarhus in the morning. Then he again saw him on post as I recall, and he said he felt as though he had nothing to lose and he was going to lay it right on him and he did lay it right on him. He told him basically what Sergeant Menzie had already related to me. He said he had it set up where the knife would be delivered to him at about 5:00, when Aarhus completed his day of duty, and he was looking for the police to be in the area so that he was covered on this thing.

"The alleged transfer was supposed to take place on Fort Devens. I suggested to him at that time that our jurisdiction was limited or nothing at all on Fort Devens and I suggested to him that he arrange a meeting at the Devens Shopping Center, which is on West Main Street in Ayer, and arrange for the transfer to take place in the Devens Shopping Center. I suggested to him that once the transfer had been made, he could start his vehicle and inadvertently hit the windshield wipers and the windshield wipers moving on the dry day would be a signal to us that the transfer had taken place, and officers in the area would converge on the truck. This was agreed upon and I hung up and immediately made a call to the district attorney's office with regard to that.

"I contacted Lt. Dwyer and advised him what had occurred and what had been arranged, and requested that he come to Ayer immediately which he did. I called the district attorney's office, as I said, and I requested the State Police officers come to Ayer and assist on this surveillance of the area and the truck. Lt. Dwyer and Trooper Keane did come to Ayer, and they were advised what had happened and what arrangements had been made. After the transaction did not take place, me, Lt. Dwyer, Trooper Keane, and Sergeant Lenny of my department, at that time, went to the CID headquarters at Fort Devens. We arrived at the CID headquarters somewhere in the vicinity of 6:00. He arrived almost simultaneously after our arrival. He was suddenly there; he was at the door. We had started to speak with the agents up there and tell them what had gone on and Mr. Tyree was there. He briefly started telling how the knife was in the barracks and he had seen it. He suggested that if we didn't get over there as soon as possible, that the knife would be gone. At that time, he did make a statement to the CID."

As the timeline began to come together concerning the events of the evening of February 13, 1979, it also began to tell a story of its own.

Since the Ayer Police Department had limited jurisdiction and the murder weapon was believed to have been kept on federal property, Chief Adamson had no choice but to involve the CID and the Massachusetts State Police. That would be the only way to get the alleged murder weapon, as it was allegedly on government property.

Special Agent Burzynski recalls, "I was notified by Chief Adamson about 5:20 that evening. He requested that I meet with him at the Fort Devens Field Office, the CID Field Office, approximately 5:30 that afternoon. Special Agent Jackson was there, Pauline Jackson was there. I called Colonel Rittgers, the post commander. We also interviewed Mr. Tyree that time at the CID Office at Fort Devens. Lt. Dwyer was there, Chief Adamson and, I believe, Special Agent Mason and Pauline Jackson, Special Agent Jackson. Tyree told me that he had been in contact with Aarhus that morning, and they had talked about the weapon used to kill Mrs. Tyree. It was about recovering that weapon from Aarhus. He came in of his own accord.

"Prior to my calling Colonel Rittgers, Specialist Tyree told me that he had been in contact with Aarhus and they had talked about recovering the weapon. He had talked about recovering the weapon from Aarhus for a sum of $5,000. And there was a meeting. He talked with Aarhus about having a meeting at the Ayer House of Pizza parking lot, where the exchange would take place. He would receive the money. Excuse me, he would receive the knife from Aarhus, and that was not agreeable with Mr. Aarhus. So, he had gone to Aarhus's room to talk over and make some other kinds of plans for receiving the weapon. He related to me that he saw the weapon in the room and this weapon was identified by Aarhus as being the weapon he had used to kill Mrs. Tyree. He also relayed that when he had left Aarhus and came to the CID office, just prior to arriving at the CID office, Aarhus appeared frightened, and he appeared as if he was shaken enough where he might try to dispose of the weapon.

"Mr. Tyree told me that part of the story he had given to Aarhus to persuade Aarhus to turn over the weapon to him was that he would get rid of the weapon by turning it over to a relative. I'm not sure whether he said uncle or cousin or whatever, and that relative would remove it from Fort Devens and take it to another state. The only thing that really comes to mind that he related to me, is that he told Aarhus that he would pay him the $5,000 upon the receipt of the insurance claim on his wife's death.

"In the presence of Lt. Dwyer and Chief Adamson and myself and, I believe, like I say, Special Agent Mason, Special Agent Jackson, Tyree came into the office and started relaying to me about an incident with this so-called deal between he and Aarhus. With that information, because of the jurisdiction of the barracks in which Aarhus's room is located, it was necessary for us to get a commander's authorization to search. So, armed with the information he had relayed to me, I called Colonel Rittgers for that purpose and sat Mr. Tyree down and had him write this document out.

"I went down to Service Company where the search was going on and placed Aarhus under apprehension, and transported him back to the CID office at Fort Devens."

Since the alleged weapon was on military property, the CID had very specific rules and regulations they had to follow. They couldn't just race up and search a building or a barracks room. They had to have first established probable cause and then convince the post commander that enough probable cause existed in order to get a search warrant authorized by the commander.

Former Post Commander Colonel Forrest Rittgers recalls the evening of February 13, 1979. He states, "I was at home. It was a little after six in the evening, about 6:10 p.m. Agent Burzynski called and stated he requested authority to search the barracks room belonging to a soldier by the name of Aarhus. He stated that he had cause to believe that the murder weapon in the Tyree case was in that room. He had interviewed Tyree and based on that interview, he had gotten a statement, I guess, from Tyree to the effect that Tyree had seen the weapon, the knife, in Aarhus's room under a pillow. So, I questioned Agent Burzynski in some detail, because what he was asking for was a telephonic authority to make a search, and this is not a normal procedure.

"Normally, I or my deputy commander, to whom I have delegated authority to authorize searches, normally we get a phone call describing circumstances and stating that an agent will be up with a written warrant for us to sign. So, we are alerted that it is coming. In this case, a written warrant had not been prepared. Due to the perishable nature of the evidence, the agent felt it was very important to get the search underway immediately, so he was requesting authority on the telephone and I questioned him in some detail about why he felt the weapon was there, what the connection was with the case, in order to establish in my mind that there was adequate probable cause to make the search.

"The written warrant was then to be executed later and signed by me later in the evening. I was going to be going off post, and I told him that and would be leaving about 7:30 p.m. and would be back somewhere around 10:30 or 11:00 p.m. So, the way we left it was that once I was satisfied that there was probable cause to make the search and authorized it, then the statement would either be prepared or signed by me prior to my departure from the post, or after I returned. I was going to be about thirty minutes away. I signed it following my return. It was shortly after eleven in the evening, in my quarters.

"I don't recall whether I phoned the CID, or notified them or not that I was back on the post, or they called me. But I probably called them. They came by my quarters and I executed the signature on it at that time. As I recall, the basic facts were the same. I would have certainly noted if they weren't, because I had questioned him in some detail about it since it was telephonic authority that I was giving, and I knew that it was very important, and I had to be certain in my own mind that there was probable cause to do that.

"Well, the major area that I questioned him on was his belief in Tyree's statement, as to whether he considered Tyree a credible witness. Why he believed him. I had to determine whether Tyree was believable to the agent, or whether he was just grasping at straws. He was very emphatic in believing what Tyree said. It was my impression that, in his dealings with Tyree, he had never felt that Tyree had been misleading him in any statements that he had taken or any associations he had with him. That was the major thrust of my questioning, was on his believing what Tyree said.

"Well, certainly my questioning of Burzynski about the credibility of Tyree, none of that is contained in the affidavit. I believe a matter of Tyree having said he saw the weapon under a pillow in the room, I believe that's contained on the backside of the written warrant. But that's what convinced me that the evidence was perishable to the point that I needed to give telephonic authority for the search, rather than going through the regular procedure. It didn't appear to me that a knife under a pillow was something that was likely to be around very long."

CID agent Paul Mason recalls, "I did receive information on that day. The 13th of February at approximately 1730 hours on that date, I had a conversation with the chief and Special Agent Burzynski at that time. That was upstairs in the polygraph room. I explained to Special Agent Burzynski to contact the operations officer within our office. This was shortly after 1730. Myself and Lt. Dwyer departed the office and went to Service Company 10th Special Forces Group to coordinate with personnel in that area.

"I arrived at the unit and identified myself as a special agent, United States Army, Special Investigation Command to the CQ who was on duty, and requested the location of the room of Aarhus and the command room. At that time, I was directed down the hallway and around the corner of the building to a room that was closed and at that time I met with the commander, Commander Polcrack.

"I attempted to locate Private Aarhus. I was unsuccessful. I then talked with the commander with reference to who was in the room and due to the fact the door was locked, I could not determine that at that time. Captain Polcrack was the company commander. He informed me that the door had not been opened and the CQ... I'm not sure whether he had the pass key with him at that time. I believe he requested to obtain the same, at that time, I'm not absolutely sure whether he came right back with it, but it was within seconds that he had the key in his hand.

"Well, prior to that, I talked with Lt. Dwyer and requested that he brief Captain Polcrack pertaining to the information that had been obtained and developed, because I was not in firsthand information of it, the information provided by Tyree.

"I went into the room and looked to see if there was anybody in there, and there wasn't. At that time, I was informed that Captain Polcrack had consented to having the room searched, him being the commander and also, I'm not absolutely sure, but I believe Miss Jackson came in and explained there was authorization in reference to the post commander authorizing a search and I picked up the pillow of the bed that had the area of Private Aarhus, and found a plastic bag containing a knife with red in color stains on it.

"The knife was confiscated as evidence and according to existing US Army Regulations, I later performed a DA Form 4137 in evidence of property received. The area was photographed. A request by Lt. Dwyer, I photographed where the knife was in the room. The pillow was on top of it and I picked it up and, as soon as I saw it, we put it down and then we photographed it."

Another party to the events was Captain Polcrack, who later recalled, "On February 13, 1979, I was commander of Service Company, 10th Special Forces Group at Fort Devens, Massachusetts. Late in the duty day that afternoon or early evening, my first sergeant, Clarence Matthews, and I were informed that military police investigators and civilian law enforcement personnel intended to conduct a search of the barracks room of Erik Aarhus, a soldier in our unit. We were asked to stand by since law enforcement personnel were in the process of presenting their probable cause information to the post commander, Colonel Forrest Rittgers, in order to obtain his permission for the search. Since Aarhus was present in the barracks at the time performing extra duty, I requested that his Parachute Rigger Section leader, Warrant Officer Ford, come to the barracks and wait with Aarhus in my office until the search was completed. It took some time for the law enforcement personnel to obtain Colonel Rittgers' permission for the search but that permission was ultimately obtained. My first sergeant and I accompanied them to Aarhus's room while Mr. Ford and Aarhus stayed in my office. The search was conducted by law enforcement personnel while my first sergeant and I observed. The primary result of the search was what appeared to me to be a bloody sheath knife wrapped in plastic, which was found under the pillow of Erik Aarhus."

Meanwhile, back at the CID office, Burzynski took Bill and placed him in a room with chicken wire, which appeared to him to be a holding cell. Then a military DA Form 4187, a personnel action that shows a soldier's change of duty status, was brought to Bill. It stated that William Tyree was taken off active duty and confined to civil authorities. This change in status occurred on February 13, 1979, at 6:20 p.m. and was signed by Service Company Commander Erik

Polcrack. This government form turned Bill over to law enforcement even before an arrest or probable cause for an arrest was made.

The timeline of February 13, 1979, based on court transcripts, reveals inconsistencies and flaws that bring the CID agents and Ayer Police officers' ethics into question:

5:40 p.m.: CID agent Burzynski called Colonel Rittgers for permission to search. (According to court transcript page 159 on 4/13/79.)

6:10 p.m.: Colonel Rittgers received a phone call from Burzynski requesting verbal permission to search. (According to handwritten notes kept by Colonel Rittgers and court transcript page 320 on 1/22/80.)

6:15 p.m.: Special Agent Mason testified that he seized the knife in Erik Aarhus's barracks room. (According to court transcript page 167-169 on 4/11/79.)

6:20 p.m.: Tyree was arrested for the first time by MPA. (According to DA Form 4187 US Army.)

6:33 p.m.: Tyree wrote a statement without his Miranda warning being read to him or an Article 831 warning. (According to court transcripts 2/25/80.)

6:40 p.m.: Burzynski called Rittgers for permission to search the barracks room. They stayed on the phone for approximately ten minutes, according to Colonel Rittgers. (According to court transcripts pages 135, 147-149, Burzynski testified that no search was underway at 6:40 p.m. pages 150-151 on 4/13/79.)

8:00 p.m.: The initial interview of Erik Aarhus began by MPA. (According to court transcripts pages 3-4 on 5/3/79.)

10:00 p.m.: Tyree was re-arrested for a second time after Aarhus allegedly confessed and incriminated Tyree. (According to the warrant and court transcripts pages 1170-

1768. Cross reference this with Tyree arrested at 6:20 p.m. in custody of MPA and confined to civil authorities.)

It was not until February 14, 1979, that Tyree was arrested with Aarhus. (According to Commonwealth v. Tyree 387 Mass 203 (1982) and Commonwealth v. Aarhus 387 Mass 735 737-739 (1982) listed 2/13/79, or the previous evening 2/12/79, as the arrest date for Tyree and Aarhus .)

***

Once Erik Aarhus was under apprehension, he was transported to the CID headquarters on post and the interrogation began. Present were Chief Adamson, Joseph Burzynski, and Massachusetts State Police lieutenant Jack Dwyer. Aarhus was read his Miranda rights and the questioning began. He stated first that Bill gave him the knife to get rid of it. He further stated that he didn't know the knife was stained with blood at first. He then claimed that he wrapped the knife in a plastic bag and threw it into the woods behind the riggers shack near Moore Army Airfield. Aarhus stated that, "I personally believe that he (Bill Tyree) didn't do it." As CID agent Burzynski put more pressure on Aarhus, the story began to change again. Burzynski started to Dutch uncle Aarhus and informed him that they didn't want him; they wanted the person who killed Elaine.

There is missing time on the tape of Aarhus's interview on the evening of February 13, 1979. Then, as soon as the police pointed out that Bill Tyree was not on Fort Devens property on February 5, 1979, but in Maryland burying his wife, the Aarhus story changed completely. He admitted to killing Elaine and being hired by Bill to do the deed. He stated that Bill drove him to the apartment to kill Elaine.

However, there were many inconsistencies with Aarhus's story. He stated that he left by the window and went through the screen. Yet the screen was not torn or ripped. Another issue was that he said he had borrowed Bill's fatigues and left them covered in blood in the apartment. Again, no bloody fatigues were found anywhere. He couldn't even tell investigators how many doors were in the apartment or what position the body was in, and this was supposedly the crime scene he was at. Aarhus said that after he left the Tyrees' apartment, he took a taxi back to the post. None of the taxi drivers recalled driving him to the post that day. It is important to remember that Erik Aarhus is of Alaskan descent and has very distinct facial features, yet the taxi drivers didn't remember seeing him at all that day. Aarhus's statement to the CID used language that was non-committal. He also used fragmented and unfinished sentences, another indication that he was withholding information. Aarhus was not very committed to any of the stories he told the CID.

When we look at the language, we have to conclude that he was being deceptive. The CID agents involved were highly trained at the expense of the American taxpayer. With all of this Training, none of them picked up on the issues I have mentioned, nor the fact that Aarhus had previously signed a false statement less than a year earlier accusing Tyree of theft. The last major issue proving Aarhus's statement to be untrue is the documented fact that he had injured his leg prior to the day of the murder. In fact, the CID had Aarhus and several other men line up and run so that an eyewitness could identify the man he saw leaving the scene on the day of the murder. But Aarhus couldn't run. The Massachusetts State Police later testified that Arhus had a cast on his leg during this time period. Bill and Erik Aarhus were then placed under arrest. Chief Adamson proceeded to the Ayer Courthouse and secured an arrest warrant for the two men, charging them both with the murder of Elaine Tyree.

The CID investigation of Elaine Tyree's murder is suspect at best. According to the Uniformed Code of Military Justice (UCMJ), when a commander learns that a subordinate is accused or suspected of committing a criminal offense, that commander is required to initiate a preliminary inquiry under Rule of Court-Martial 303. Immediately upon learning of the murder, Tyree was placed under guard, but Commander Cutolo never initiated an inquiry, which would have been followed up with an Article 32 hearing. This hearing is a proceeding similar to a civilian preliminary hearing in which the convening authority will usually consult with command and judge advocate for advice on case disposition. This decides whether there is enough evidence to proceed with a court-martial or dismiss the charges. This was never done. Even though the murder took place off post, the CID should have taken the lead role in this case. This is because the CID can investigate even when there is a civilian law enforcement interest or involvement in the investigation as long as the reason for the CID investigation is to satisfy army investigative needs in a criminal matter of army interest. It seems to me that the murder of a soldier and the finding of the alleged murder weapon on government property should be a matter of army interest.

When the CID found the knife, they never sealed off the barracks or the surrounding area to question who may have seen something or had access to Aarhus's barracks room. The knife should have been sent to the FBI lab for processing, not turned over to civilian authorities. The CID never fingerprinted the barracks room to see who else may have been in there. During their questioning, Aarhus and Tyree were not informed of their rights or given access to a lawyer. Aarhus gave his statement while under the influence of powerful narcotics, which should make any statement he gave suspect. The CID didn't take ordinary investigative steps to determine if or how the barracks room had changed prior to their arrival. The CID recklessly represented to Colonel Rittgers that a thorough investigation had been conducted, which was not true. The CID's mistakes are so numerous and their omissions and outright misstatements of fact are so egregious that the record needs to be set straight. The CID never developed a motive and assumed it was not significant to investigate until Aarhus made one up in his statement. They recklessly conducted interviews using character assassination techniques and never evaluated the results.

These CID agents perjured testimony and suppressed evidence, which constitutes possible conduct unbecoming of officers and/or conduct which is prejudicial to good order and discipline, and brought disgrace to the army.

In 1982, Chief Adamson testified in a deposition for a matter related to this case:

Question: Did you have the opportunity to speak to a lieutenant in the United States Army that lived in that building at 104 1/2 Washington Street?

Adamson: Yes. Yes, there was a lieutenant who was interviewed.

Question: And specifically, that lieutenant told you, did he not, that on that particular day in question, at that particular time, he held the door open for William Tyree alone with a baby carriage in his arms, isn't that correct?

Adamson: Yes, that's correct.

Question: Did he also tell you that he didn't see anybody else?

Adamson: That's what he said.

Question: And yet, Erik Aarhus told you that he and Tyree were together, isn't that correct? He said Mr. Tyree admitted him to that apartment. And the lieutenant said Tyree was alone, correct?

Adamson: When he observed him, yes.

With all these facts in place, the CID and the Ayer Police Department looked no further than Erik Aarhus and Bill Tyree for Elaine's murder and placed both men under arrest. Bill and Erik were booked and processed, then sent up to Middlesex County Jail and House of Correction in Billerica, Massachusetts. It is important to further note that Chief Adamson was never held accountable for his previous actions of omission concerning an eyewitness account of Tyree being alone that day at the apartment. This is definitely suppression of evidence that would clearly raise the question of reasonable doubt. There was also a witness who saw someone running through the apartment complex on the day and around the time the murder occurred. The witness was Vias Williams, a soldier assigned to Fort Devens who lived in an apartment within the complex where the Tyree family resided.

In a 1997 interview Williams recalled, "There was nothing unusual that day when I got home. I walked into the apartment, took off my coat, talked to my wife for a few minutes, and went over to the couch to play with my son, who was about three months old lying on the couch. In front of the couch was a picture window. Curtains were open, it was a pretty sunshiny clear day, but it was cold, being January. I noticed somebody running behind my apartment, which the ground was snow-covered and kind of icy. So, it caught my attention. That's when I saw a man probably six feet with dark hair and kind of stocky running behind my building. I didn't get a look at his face because I was on the second floor, which probably was twelve foot up. I didn't think much of it and continued eating my lunch and departed sometime around 12:30. When I got in my car and started to back out, I noticed a screen on the first-floor apartment was laying against the side of the building, which wasn't there or didn't catch my eye when I came home for lunch. There was no other activity outside the buildings and nobody was going to work, no police cars or anything else around."

Mr. Williams' recollection is unique for two reasons. First, the man he saw running was six foot tall. Aarhus is barely five foot, four inches, and the screen to the Tyrees' apartment window was on the ground prior to the Ayer Police Department's arrival, which is contrary to what the responding Ayer Police officer would later testify to.

Bill recalls, "On February 13, 1979, at 1820 hours, although placed under arrest first by Lt. Jack Dwyer of the Massachusetts State Police, I was not given my Miranda rights until after 2100 hours (9:00 p.m.). I did request that since I was on Fort Devens, under jurisdiction of the US Army, that Judge Advocate General Staff Captain Daniel Carrigan be allowed to speak to me before I wrote the statement. Lt. Dwyer refused that request for counsel and told me to cooperate with Agent Burzynski and I wouldn't get into any trouble. Also contrary to the statement I allegedly made, I did not and have not any time ever seen a knife under the Service Company barracks pillow of Erik Y. Aarhus and I will take a polygraph test to prove that."

"I have never seen a major trial which lacked significant perjury, and I have yet to see that perjury punished." F. Lee Bailey

CHAPTER FIVE

HANO: High Altitude No Opening

The following day, February 14,1979, Earl Michael Peters went into the CID headquarters and informed CID agent Paul Mason that he wanted to make a statement against Bill Tyree. Mason led him into an interrogation room and listened to what he had to say. When Peters was finished, Mason gave him a CID Form AR 190-45, which is used for a sworn statement.

Peters proceeded to write, "Sometime on a Sunday morning early in November 1978, at approximately 1000 hours, I was with PVT William Tyree in his truck, which at that time was located adjacent to his quarters in Ayer, Massachusetts. We were going to go hunting and he was asking how good of a shot I was. He asked me if I could hit a moving target or a vehicle moving at 55 MPH. He then asked me if I could shoot his wife if she was in his truck on the 495 going toward New Hampshire. He said he would call it the mad sniper attack. I told him that I thought he was crazy. He didn't offer me any money. I believe he was feeling me out because he used the word 'if' a number of times. The next time we had a talk about killing his wife was around the 3rd or on the 10th of December, 1978. Again, we were in the parking lot of his house and he was fixing some speakers in his vehicle. He was asking me how to get to the White Mountains in an area where a man had rolled his truck and died as a result of the accident. I told him how to get there and he said it would be great if his wife would get hurt or killed in a similar accident."

Peters' statement continued, "On the 28th of January, 1979, I was in the latrine of my unit and I observed Tyree with Aarhus getting into a vehicle. I called out a window and asked Tyree where they were going, and he told me they were going to negotiate." Peters continued on and told Mason in his statement about how Bill thought Aarhus committed the crime because of the diaries Elaine was keeping. Earl Michael Peters signed the statement along with CID agent Paul Mason and witness CID agent Joseph Burzynski. Never once did either agent raise the question of why Peters was coming forward now, after Tyree had been arrested. Most people who hear someone make statements of the type that he was alleging would have informed Elaine or someone prior to the murder.

Dennis Testagrossa was interviewed on February 13, 1979, by CID agent Joseph Burzynski at the CID office on post. CID Form 94 states: "PFC Testagrossa was questioned pertaining to any conversations which may have occurred between him and PVT Tyree. PFC Testagrossa related that approximately 1200 hours, February 1, 1979, he had accompanied PVT Tyree to the post exchange, Fort Devens, Massachusetts. He further provided that while they were at the PX PVT, Tyree met a service member described as an SGT or SFC belonging to the 10th Special Forces Group (A). He further provided that this service member was accompanied by a female, apparently a civilian. PFC Testagrossa continued that PVT Tyree related to the male service member the incidents of his wife's murder. PFC Testagrossa continued that the incident was relayed to the service member that PVT Tyree's wife had been surprised by a male when she entered the apartment in Ayer, MA. Reportedly, the male was hiding behind the front door in an alcove section of the hall and when his wife realized the individual was present, she exchanged words with him. The conversation continued that his wife attempted to run away from the male, at which time she was stabbed in the right arm while the male was standing behind her. Then he reportedly stabbed her twice in the back, causing her to fall to the floor. The conversation continued that the man rolled her onto her back and continued stabbing her in the chest area approximately three to four times and then cut her throat. PFC Testagrossa stated that during the conversation, Tyree related to the service member that one of the injuries inflicted upon his wife was so deep that it passed completely through her body. Tyree stated that a neighbor living in the same housing complex saw a male jump from the apartment window and run from the area while the police were knocking at the front door. PFC Testagrossa was able to relate to this agent another incident which occurred while he was accompanying Tyree during the aforementioned period. He stated Tyree told him that the person who committed the murder must have known Tyree and his wife because of the conversation overheard by the neighbor."

After the search of Aarhus's barracks room, US Army Form AR 340-15 states that: "Bloody clothing was recovered as well as the knife and 300 to 400 blue tablets. The tablets were later discovered to be diazepam, which had a street value of $300 dollars. Upon further questioning, Aarhus informed the CID that he had received the tablets from another soldier."

According to the army form, the soldier was apprehended at 0700 hours on February 15, 1979, and was charged with wrongful possession of a controlled substance and sale of a controlled substance. After he was processed, he was released to his unit. The form was signed by Captain Stephan V. Ottesen.

This military form is the only mention of bloody clothes or drugs being found in the search of Aarhus's barracks room. Neither the pre-trial nor the trial entered or mentioned bloody clothes into evidence and Aarhus was never charged with possession of a controlled substance or attempted distribution. Any person being found with that number of pharmaceuticals would have been charged along with the murder of Elaine Tyree. Furthermore, the finding of drugs should have brought into question Aarhus's state of mind when he made the statement. The 0700 hours apprehension time, arrest, and release to unit on February 15, 1979, should raise red flags. After all, Aarhus was already placed under arrest and in custody of civilian authorities approximately twenty-seven hours earlier. This is verified through prison records and court documents. So, how could he have been arrested by the military and released back to his unit when he was already in custody?

Then there is the question of the alleged blood-stained clothing taken from the room and listed in the inventory. What size was the clothing? Were the stains really from blood and if so, was the blood type the same as the blood type on the knife found in the same room? The fact that the clothing and pills were never mentioned or brought forth as evidence in either trial is highly suspect. A defense attorney would definitely have been able to get the entire room search thrown out on the basis of the break in the chain of custody as well as the highly questionable confession. This is due to the case being solely hinged on the fact that the above evidence was all tainted fruit from the same tree.

On February 15, 1979, Massachusetts State Police interviewed Dennis Testagrossa. Chief William Adamson of the Ayer Police and CID agent Joseph Burzynski were also present at the interview.

Burzynski asked, "During the conversation with either Captain Cote or with this service member at the PX, you mentioned to me yesterday that when Tyree was talking about a neighbor seeing somebody jump out the window, you told me that Tyree had stated that the person was seen jumping out the window of the apartment while the policeman was at the front door."

Testagrossa replied, "Okay. While the police were either getting there or at the front door. He said while the police were at the front door. He said that somebody, I guess a neighbor, saw somebody jumping out a window."

The rest of the interview was based on what Testagrossa had reported to the CID the day before.

***

The Ayer Police, the CID, and the Massachusetts State Police now believed that they had enough evidence against Bill Tyree and Erik Aarhus to present to the Middlesex District Attorney's Office to warrant their arrests and prosecution. However, the Middlesex District Attorney's Office felt that the case was circumstantial at best and decided to have a probable cause hearing. This would take place at the Ayer District Courthouse. A judge would be assigned to hear sworn testimony from any and all witnesses who were subpoenaed by the prosecutor or the defendant's attorney. The purpose of the hearing was to establish that first, a crime had been committed, and Second, that the defendant had committed it. This hearing occurred after the first grand jury refused to indict Bill either for murder or as an accessory.

Once Bill Tyree was arrested, his mother and father immediately made plans to come to Massachusetts. They wanted to be there both emotionally and physically for Bill. They wanted to ensure that if there was anything he needed, they would be able to help him. Once they realized that this was not going to be over with quickly, Gaye Tyree began looking for a house to rent in or around Ayer.

On April 3, 1979, a probable cause hearing was convened at the Ayer District Courthouse. The Honorable James Killam III presided over the proceedings. Special Judge Killam III was a mild-mannered man who stood at about five foot, eleven inches, with brownish hair and a mustache. He normally sat on the bench at Malden District Court but had been brought in especially for this case. He had a reputation for being tough but fair, which was exactly what this case needed. Unlike a grand jury proceeding, this hearing permitted participation by both prosecution and defense counsels, with Judge Killam functioning as judge and jury.

The probable cause hearing started out like any other. The witnesses were sequestered as per the defendant's request. On the first couple days, the witnesses testified as to the events leading up to the discovery of Elaine's body and Bill Tyree's actions at the funeral. The first witnesses were the Gibsons, Chief Adamson, and officers of the Ayer Police Department.

Then Earl Michael Peters testified. This witness testimony changed everything. Peters' first day of testimony centered on the statement he had made to the CID on February 14, 1979. They were attempting to clarify what exactly Bill Tyree had allegedly said to Peters about soliciting him to kill his wife.

The second day of testimony, Peters spoke about who Tyree thought may have killed his wife. He stated, "I asked him who he thought did it and he told me Erik Aarhus. I asked him why, and he said that Erik Aarhus had been over to his apartment the night before she was killed, trying to obtain a little blue book that contained information concerning some of the people in the unit, mostly about the riggers."

Further on in his testimony, Peters recalled being asked if he had a Remington 1100 shotgun. He stated, "It's at my home right now. It was under the couch at the Tyrees' apartment. On the 28th of January, I was over at Bill's house and his wife and he were arguing. It was a Saturday or a Sunday. If it was a Sunday then it was a Sunday. I can't remember which. But I did remove the Remington 1100 from his house. I checked it in the next morning, immediately after 7:00 a.m. formation. When I turned in the weapon to the arms room I received a receipt, which I no longer have."

Peters went into further detail about why he kept the weapon at Bill's house. "I put it there because it was easy access for me to get because of the late duck season that was coming in New Hampshire. If I kept it in the arms room, I would have had to go through the first sergeant and a lot of paperwork and stuff. Sometimes I couldn't get it because I couldn't get the time off from work to get down to the first sergeant to get the company armor to open the arms room up. Suppose it was a weekend and I couldn't keep the rifle in the billets overnight, and that's why I kept it at Bill's house."

The defense attorney also addressed the skill Peters had acquired from all his years of hunting. He questioned Peters extensively on the procedures of hunting, even getting graphic as to the proper way to slit an animal's throat so as to drain the blood. Peters gave a reason for his removal of the weapon. "I was going on leave or on pass, rather, on Wednesday, and I was going to leave Tuesday night. The other reason was that Bill and Elaine were packing to go to Utah and that's why the shotgun was removed and put in the arms room."

The defense attorney even presented crime scene photographs of the Tyree apartment. In the pictures, the couch was tipped and in the open position to display the storage area below it. The square storage space under the couch that had been previously occupied by the green and white shotgun box containing Peters' shotgun could be seen in the photographs. This raised questions as to the possibility of someone retrieving the gun during the murder. During his testimony, Peters admitted to owning thirty knives and seventeen rifles.

Judge Killam immediately believed that Peters' testimony had been coached. Peters testified that Bill and SP4 Johnson had come to the Service Company day room on January 31 and got him out of class. Tyree informed him that he needed clothes because the police were investigating his home and he was in PT clothes. Peters then lent him some fatigues. Peters claimed that he learned of Elaine's death from a lieutenant right after 7:00 a.m. formation on Wednesday, January 31, 1979. Then he went on leave to his home in Pennsylvania and brought his shotgun with him.

According to his testimony, Peters went to the apartment on January 28 to retrieve his Remington 1100 semi-automatic with a chamber for a three-inch magazine. The shotgun was stored in a box measuring four feet long, six feet wide, and two inches high. The box had the name "Remington" on it. Peters claimed he kept the gun in his wall locker on Sunday until the arms room was opened on Monday morning, when he could check it in. When Wayne Maxon, the unit armorer for Service Company 10th Group, and Lieutenant Hall took inventory of the arms room on January 30, 1979, the inventory sheet showed only one private weapon: a Remington 1100 serial number N-000929M checked in on January 29, at 9:30 a.m. However, Peters testified in Tyree's 1980 trial that the serial number to his weapon was 0214619. A hand receipt for the weapon was also miraculously recovered from the trash two weeks after it was thrown out. Maxon testified about the entry on the arms room sheet of Peters' shotgun being signed in on an earlier date than the murder. Something seemed off and the lawyers quickly picked up on this issue, as did Judge Killam III.

Bill recalls, "Peters was done testifying and starts to step off the witness stand and you hear this voice from the bench say, 'Mr. Peters. I have some questions for you. Remain on the stand.' Assistant District Attorney DeMichaelis jumps up and goes, 'Your Honor, I am done with him.' Judge Killam replies, 'I'm just beginning!' I've seen Peters squirm before. But this time he looked like a fish trying to get free of a hook. He knew that Judge Killam was taking off the gloves. All through the examination of Peters, the attorneys just never went into certain areas. No one knows why. They just didn't go there. Well, Judge Killam went there in a big way. He ran over Peters like the Indians ran over Custer. There were no survivors."

Peters claimed that on the day of the murder he had been sleeping in his barracks room because he worked at the motor pool from 4:30 a.m. till Monday morning at approximately 8:30 or 9:00 a.m. His roommates even testified to the same. However, their testimony was suspect because Peters was feared by the soldiers he shared a room with.

During the hearing there was a bench conference between Judge Killam, Mr. DeMichaelis, and Mr. Spadafora. The conference went as follows:

The court: We are all big boys, right? It's entirely possible that Peters is the knife man.

Mr. Spadafora: I think you're right; I really do.

Mr. DeMichaelis: All that I know…

The court: That's off the record completely.

On May 7, 1979, William Tyree was indicted for murder. The very next day, in a second sitting of the grand jury, Assistant District Attorney Dante DeMichaelis, per agreement with attorney Bernard Bradley, trial counsel notified District Court Judge Killam, sitting by appointment on the probable cause hearing, that the district attorney wouldn't seek a grand jury indictment or take any action against Tyree until the probable cause hearing verdict was rendered by Judge Killam. However, unbeknownst to anyone, Assistant District Attorney John Kerry, who would later serve as United States Secretary of State, had presented evidence to a grand jury alleging that Bill had beaten his wife to death. This secret indictment charging murder under Massachusetts General Law Chapter 265 Section 1, was handed down from the grand jury on May 7, 1979, eight days before Judge Killam's decision. As a side note, it did take the Commonwealth of Massachusetts two tries before securing the indictment. Well, so much for gentlemen's agreements.

The next witness to be called was CID agent Joseph Burzynski. Almost immediately, Burzynski was evasive and nervous, referring to his notes for even the most routine of questions. He answered basic questions about the interview conducted at CID headquarters with Earl Michael Peters. His testimony didn't reveal any new information for either side.

Colonel Forrest Rittgers Jr., the Commander of Fort Devens, testified:

DeMichaelis: And in your capacity as the commander of the post, whether or not you had the authority, just as a magistrate has, to issue warrants and authority to search?

Rittgers: I do.

DeMichaelis: Would you relate to us, in substance, the information which Agent Burzynski conveyed to you at that time?

Rittgers: Agent Burzynski called and stated he requested authority to search the barracks room belonging to a soldier by the name of Aarhus. He stated that he had cause to believe that the murder weapon in the Tyree case was in that room.

DeMichaelis: And did he give you information as to why he had cause to believe that that murder weapon... By the way, did he indicate what kind of a murder weapon it was?

Rittgers: A knife.

DeMichaelis: Did he indicate to you what the factors were that caused him to believe that the murder weapon was there?

Rittgers: He had gotten a statement, I guess, from when he had interviewed Tyree, to the effect that Tyree had seen the weapon, the knife, in Aarhus's room, under a pillow. So, I questioned Agent Burzynski in some detail, because what he was asking for was a telephonic authority to make a search, and this is not a normal procedure. Normally, I or my deputy commander, whom I have delegated authority to, also to authorize searches, normally we get a phone call describing circumstances and stating that an agent will be up with a written warrant for us to sign. So, we are alerted that it is coming. In this case, a written warrant had not been prepared. Due to the perishable nature of the evidence, the agent felt it was very important to get the search underway immediately, so he was requesting authority on the telephone and I questioned him in some detail about why he felt the weapon was there, what the connection was with the case, in order to establish in my mind that there was adequate probable cause to make the search. The written warrant was then to be executed later, and signed by me later in the evening. I was going to be going off post, and I told him that and would be leaving about 7:30 p.m. and would be back somewhere around 10:30 or 11:00 p.m. So, the way we left it was that once I was satisfied that there was probable cause to make the search and authorized it, then the statement would either be prepared and signed by me prior to my departure from the post, or after I returned. I was going to be about thirty minutes away. I signed it following my return. It was shortly after 11:00 in the evening, in my quarters. I don't recall whether I phoned the CID or notified them or not that I was back on the post, or they called me. But I probably called them. They came by my quarters and I executed the signature on it at that time.

DeMichaelis: And prior to your signing it, whether or not you read the entire affidavit and attachments?

Rittgers: Yes, sir, I did.

DeMichaelis: And whether or not anything that appeared on that warrant was not conveyed to you telephonically, prior thereto, on the occasion of Agent Burzynski calling?

Rittgers: As I recall, the basic facts were the same. I would have certainly noted if they weren't, because I had questioned him in some detail about it since it was telephonic authority that I was giving, and I knew that it was very important, and I had to be certain in my own mind that there was probable cause to do that.

DeMichaelis: Whether at that time you were aware that Tyree was the husband of an alleged victim in the case, that his wife was a deceased person?

Rittgers: Oh, yes.

DeMichaelis: And some of these questions that you questioned him about in detail, can you recall some of those questions?

Rittgers: Well, the major area that I questioned him on was his belief in Tyree's statement, as to whether he considered him a credible witness. Why he and I believed him. I had to determine whether Tyree was believable to the agent, or whether he was just grasping at straws.

DeMichaelis: What was his response to that?

Rittgers: He was very emphatic in believing what Tyree said. It was my impression that, in his dealings with Tyree, he had never felt that Tyree had been misleading him in any statements that he had taken or any associations he had had with him. That was the major thrust of my questioning, was on his believing what Tyree said.

DeMichaelis: What time was it that the written warrant, affidavit and attachments, were brought to you?

Rittgers: About 11:15. My memo of that night indicates 11:15.

DeMichaelis: Do you know whether or not they had just completed the written warrant by that time?

Rittgers: I don't know. I don't know what time it was done. It may be on that. That wasn't part of our discussion.

DeMichaelis: I show you these documents. I show you these documents, Colonel, and ask you whether or not you recognize those?

Rittgers: I recognize the first three pages. I don't recall seeing the pages in long hand. I don't have any recollection of seeing that. I have a copy. I have my own copy, which is normal, of the first three pages. Every time I execute a warrant, I am given a copy of that portion, so I have this and am familiar with these three pages. But I don't recall that this was attached to it at the time that I signed on it.

DeMichaelis: I refer you to the third page and ask you to read that portion, and whether or not that... I'm sorry, wait a minute, read this portion, whether or not that refreshes your recollection as to whether there was a written portion attached to the other documents?

Rittgers: Well, this states a copy of Tyree's statement is attached in support of this affidavit. However, I didn't sign this affidavit. I signed this page here. This affidavit is signed, sworn to by the superior of Agent Burzynski, so that would have had to have been attached at the time it was sworn to before Mr. Collins. When I signed the first page, certainly the typed document was attached to it. I don't recall a written statement being with it. I just don't recall one way or the other. Can I read this?

DeMichaelis: Yes.

More questioning ensued. The interview continued:

DeMichaelis: Colonel, can you tell me exactly at time Agent Burzynski called you at your home on the night of the 13th?

Rittgers: 1610 hours.

DeMichaelis: Which is 4:10 p.m.?

Rittgers: That's correct.

DeMichaelis: You testified that you questioned him at great length, you know, concerning what was his probable cause. Is this true?

Rittgers: Yes, sir.

DeMichaelis: Can you tell me how long that conversation took place?

Rittgers: No.

DeMichaelis: You said great lengths. To what is great lengths? Do you have any idea?

Rittgers: The reason I said great lengths is that I had the feeling that Agent Burzynski wanted to get on with his business, and I was holding him up with my questions.

DeMichaelis: I have that feeling too. That's why I want to know how long this conversation was.

Rittgers: I didn't check my watch when I finished. It could have been five minutes, or it could have been ten minutes. It could have been fifteen minutes.

It is interesting to note that during Colonel Rittgers' questioning of CID agent Burzynski, he said Agent Burzynski stated that he felt that PVT Tyree was being honest with him and had never been misleading in his interactions with him. This is rather strange, since Burzynski had a prior relationship with Tyree and felt he was uncooperative during the Article 15 debacle. Could this be CID agent Burzynski recklessly embellishing the facts to get authorization to search after the fact, since the agent's timeline and the colonel's timeline don't match up? If the colonel's timeline is correct, then the agents did the search without prior authorization.

The next day, Bill Tyree's friend, Michael Menzie, was called to the stand. He testified to the kind of relationship Bill and Elaine had. The most interesting part of his testimony is as follows: "He (Bill) told me he wanted to talk to me alone, and we went into the hallway, and he said that he had a problem and that people were trying to get him. He said that somebody would try to get him, and the only way they could get him was through Elaine and the baby. At the time I didn't believe him. He said he wanted to get Elaine out of the area and that nobody would back him up." Menzie further testified, "In the middle of the night, he would hear someone turning the knob or messing with the key place. I had to go back on post to pick something up because I was working on this thing and Bill gave me a ride. While we were gone, Elaine showed my girlfriend how easy it actually was to break into their apartment door."

Bill recalls the probable cause hearing. "The one thing that really sticks out in my mind about the probable cause hearing... Well, actually there are two things. Chief Adamson was warned by Judge Killam not to coach any more of the sequestered witnesses such as Bruce Beechum and Mary Burton, and Judge Killam questioned Peters for nearly six hours! All the witnesses were sequestered...

except Chief Adamson, who was allowed to sit with the district attorney and answer any questions the D.A. had. We clocked him doing it. The judge was alerted to this fact and then it happened. Chief Adamson got his first warning from Judge Killam, 'Don't coach the witnesses.' Now, most people would stop their conduct if a judge warned them. But Adamson had an ego the size of the courthouse and sure enough, the second case of witness tampering appeared.

"Mary Burton testified the first day and her testimony wasn't too bad. The next day, she is back and this time she had remembered something that tore me apart. Of course, I never did what she said I did the second time she testified, but she got it on the record. So, I told my attorney, Mr. Bradley, he had to prove she was lying and sure enough, when it's all said and done, she admitted that Chief Adamson had called her overnight between the first and second time she testified. Adamson suggested that she may have heard something that in the end, she admitted she had not heard. So, the judge lets Mary Burton leave and has Adamson stand up.

"Judge Killam gives him the third degree and down Adamson goes, and low and behold, in walks Bruce Beechum. Beechum had testified the day before also and now had startling new information. He remembered it in his sleep. Mr. Bradley gives me the old 'you've got to be joking' look as he stands up shaking his head back and forth, smiling at Judge Killam. Bradley says, 'Don't tell me, and let me guess? Last night the chief of police called and said that Mr. Tyree was going to get away with murdering his wife. That is, unless you come forward with something else. Then the chief said something like, did Mr. Tyree ever do or do this, or that, maybe this.' In the end, Bruce Beechum admitted that the chief had 'suggested' that Beechum might add a few things to his testimony. Right before the witness is excused, the courtroom is packed and you can hear a pin drop. Adamson is told to stand up and the best part of the probable cause hearing took place."

The following is direct from the probable cause hearing transcript:

Judge Killam: Chief, do you know where the Billerica House of Correction is? Because if you don't, I suggest that you find out. Because if one more witness takes the stand and tells this court that you suggested they amend or change their testimony, you're going to Billerica with Mr. Tyree. Do I make myself clear?

Adamson never even blinked. He didn't even apologize to the court or imply that the witnesses may have misunderstood his instructions. Instead, he just looked shocked that the judge had challenged him and exposed him, while a packed courtroom snickered. No charges were ever filed against Chief Adamson.

Tyree's lawyer should have been astute enough to raise this issue later on at trial and show that witness tampering and collusion had taken place, thereby completely discrediting the Ayer Police Department and their investigative findings.

On May 15,1979, after some thirty-five witnesses testified and were questioned by both counsel and judge, the decision was announced—the very same day the results of a secretly conducted grand jury were announced by the Middlesex County District Attorney. Because the two proceedings reached diametrically opposite conclusions, that disconnect was then and continues to be the subject of significant controversy.

The decision by Judge Killam III shocked the parties who had a vested interest in this case. The decision reads as follows:

"That the evidence ought to be taken in the light most favorable to the prosecution and that ordinary questions of credibility in the usual probable cause hearing appears to be settled law. However, the emergence of the alleged murder weapon with the blood of the victim still on it, preserved in two plastic bags and found under the pillow of the defendant (Aarhus) charged with the deed; which barracks are vulnerable to daily inspections would strain the credibility of even the most gullible. The enlightened suspicion of 'frame' is inescapable.

"The defendant, Tyree, had two best friends. First, Staff Sgt. Menzie had nothing but concern for Tyree and his wife, Elaine, to the extent that Staff Sgt. Menzie all but forced Tyree to go through with a listing of suspects and circumstances. These, Tyree failed to produce. Second, Special 4 Earl Michael Peters, a regular visitor at the Tyree apartment, had the confidence of William Tyree and his intimate knowledge of the Tyrees' home and habits together with his probable involvement with Tyree in various illegal activities suggests his involvement in the homicide. This same intimacy tends to explain Tyree's apparently accurate grasp of the events surrounding his wife's death. Peters' obvious guile and Tyree's apparent intellectual deficiency (as adduced from the testimony of most witnesses) lead more believably toward Peters leading and Tyree's following in various disclosures and discoveries subsequent to the homicide."

Judge Killam went on to state, "I feel compelled to comment upon three pieces of demonstrative evidence which I believed to have been manufactured to bolster a marginally credible proposition in sequence of events. These are the three hand receipts, two for Peters' Remington 1100 auto loading shotgun and one for defendant Aarhus's Buck 105 Pathfinder sheath type hunting knife. The customarily entered serial number of the shotgun was not entered on the receipts which conveniently turned up in the arms room trash can, which conveniently had not been emptied in two weeks preceding a government interview with the armorer. The receipt for Aarhus's hunting knife is dated on a day in December of 1978, when there is no record of entry into the arms room and which emerged from the hip pocket of the armorer during his testimony on the witness stand."

Bill remembers, "The probable cause hearing was a dog and pony show, to say the least. It was wall to wall standing room only. The first murder in that area in over twenty years, and people turned out because the newspapers were having a slow year. The papers played it up for all it was worth. Every rumor, every fact, every quote. It was all there in the local papers. They tore the case apart. Tore me apart. Tore Aarhus apart. Tore the cops apart. Tore Judge Killam apart. Then did it several more times for good luck. Then in the blink of an eye that all changed. I went from being a scumbag that killed his wife to the poor husband the judge said didn't do it. Headlines actually read after I was indicted and the indictment was revealed to the public: 'Tyree indicted despite judge's contrary decision.'

"The grand jury never knew about the decision of Judge Killam. It's either feast or famine in America. Either you did it or you didn't do it! They hate you today and love you tomorrow. It's nothing more than peer pressure. No one wants to be an individual anymore. It's herd mentality. Survival of the smartest. The dumb are doomed and don't realize it. As more skull-doggery surfaced of an exculpatory nature, the more press I finally began to receive. By the time the probable cause was over, I already had seen the mood swing into my favor. They stopped spitting at the police car as I rode by inside of it. Of course, spitting at the crooked cops in my case, it's hard to tell if they were spitting at the cops or at me. The cops found no humor in it either."

Judge Killam stated, "In view of the foregoing, together with and after complete hearing of all the evidence, all parties being represented by counsel and with full opportunity to be heard and to examine witnesses, I make the following determinations and orders:

Pvt. William Tyree. Probable cause found and complaints of process to issue if not already issued.

1. Accessory after the fact of murder.

2. Conspiracy with Earl Michael Peters to obstruct justice.

3. Obstruction of justice.

Pvt. Erik V. Aarhus. Probable cause found and complaint and process to issue if not already issued.

1. Accessory before the fact of murder.

2. Murder in the first degree.

3. Conspiracy with Earl Michael Peters to murder Elaine Tyree.

Spec. 4 Earl Michael Peters. I hereby order Chief William Adamson Sr. or his designee to execute the following complaints against Earl Michael Peters, without further obligation as a result of this order and I hereby order Warren Birch, Esq. Clerk, or his designee to issue process as a result thereof against the said Earl Michael Peters.

1. Accessory before the fact of murder.

2. Accessory after the fact of murder.

3. Conspiracy with Erik V. Aarhus to murder.

4. Murder of Elaine Tyree in the first degree.

5. Conspiracy with William Tyree to obstruct justice.

6. Obstruction of justice.

No probable cause found on complaints not enumerated.

I further hereby decline jurisdiction of any charges otherwise appropriate to the District Court Department and further hereby notify any and all defendants of their right to waive indictment and to proceed to trial upon the foregoing complaints."

After Judge Killam read his findings to the court, the following conversation took place in the court:

Judge Killam: No, I am charging Tyree as an accessory after the fact of murder, being in conspiracy with Earl Michael Peters to obstruct justice, and with plain old obstruction of justice.

ADA Dante DeMichaelis: Why? May I inquire as to why these charges are brought against Mr. Tyree?

Judge Killam: Sure! I'm convinced that Mr. Tyree figured some of this out and didn't tell anyone what he knew. Now, I don't know if Mr. Tyree didn't cooperate with Chief Adamson because Tyree didn't trust him, or if Tyree intended to take matters into his own hands. The evidence would lend itself to Mr. Tyree having more knowledge than he is letting onto. That would make him guilty of obstructing justice if convicted of the crime. I added accessory after the fact and conspiracy because I don't know what Mr. Tyree does. Until Mr. Tyree has a chance to explain this to a jury, I would charge all three and let a jury make the decision on how they want to proceed.

ADA DeMichaelis: I don't think you can do that. Can you? I mean, I've never seen that done before.

Judge Killam: I just did it! Process the complaints! Is that going to be a problem?

ADA DeMichaelis: I'm going to have to call the district attorney first. May I have leave of the court to place that call?

Judge Killam: Process the complaints first.

Bernard Bradley, Bill Tyree's defense attorney: Your Honor, may I be heard?

Judge Killam: As long as it has nothing to do with the fresh complaints I have brought against your client.

Bernard Bradley: It does.

Judge Killam: What is it?

Bernard Bradley: Can you do that? I understand the charges against Mr. Aarhus and even Mr. Peters, but I don't believe that the hearing produced any evidence against Mr. Tyree to support these new charges.

Judge Killam: Perhaps you are right, but a hearing on the charges would certainly clear the air regarding any involvement by Mr. Tyree.

Bernard Bradley: Is the court implying that a hearing should be held to determine if Mr. Tyree committed any of those crimes you have alleged?

Judge Killam: Yes! It would provide Mr. Tyree with an opportunity to explain himself and remove any doubts from the minds of those that know Mr. Tyree. It would give him a chance to be heard.

Bernard Bradley: Mr. Tyree has informed me that he has no problem with the new charges. Is Mr. Tyree still being considered in any other charges before this court?

Judge Killam: No."

At this point, Bill and his attorney, Bernard Bradley, believed he would be released pending a new probable cause hearing, until they learned of the secret grand jury indictment that had been handed down eight days earlier. Bill and Aarhus never left the custody of the Commonwealth of Massachusetts. In order to conceal the probable cause hearing and Judge Killam's decision of May 15, 1979, from Tyree's future jury trial and to conceal the promise not to indict Tyree or take action against him until Judge Killam rendered the probable cause hearing decision, District

Attorney Droney sued the court. This can be found in Killam via GLC 211.

The first piece of evidence that fell under scrutiny was the knife being found late in the afternoon on February 13, 1979, two weeks after Elaine Tyree was murdered. It was found wrapped in one or two plastic bags and under Erik Aarhus's pillow. The knife clearly belonged to Aarhus and had blood thereon matching Elaine's blood type. No DNA analysis was then available or has been provided since. The enlightened suspicion of a frame up is inescapable. What are the probabilities that a young Special Forces soldier trained in the arts of bodily offense and defense would:

1. Retain for two weeks a severely soiled knife?

2. Retain for two weeks a knife soiled with blood?

3. Retain for two weeks a knife soiled with human blood?

4. Retain for two weeks a knife soiled with the blood of a victim who was allegedly murdered by the owner of the knife?

5. Store that knife in an open, unsecure area subject to random discovery?

6. Do any of these things while the knifes owner is a person of interest in a murder investigation by military and civilian authorities?

The only piece of forensic evidence arguably connecting Aarhus with the murder was the knife. Apparently, some two percent of the general population have Type B blood, which was found on his knife, and without DNA analysis an informed prosecutor might well be reluctant to proceed against Erik Aarhus, absent more compelling evidence. Worse still, no fingerprints of Aarhus could be found on the knife or on the plastic bag from a delicatessen that contained the knife at its discovery, despite being in the possession of the Commonwealth for some two months. Nor were attempts made to pursue the origin of the plastic bag.

The second piece of evidence that came under inquiry was the testimony of Sergeant Michael Menzie. During the probable cause hearing, Menzie's testimony was twisted by the Commonwealth to assist in confirming Tyree's guilt. However, once Assistant District Attorney DeMichaelis began his direct examination of Menzie, he began to elicit statements that moved away from the intent of the prosecution. The Commonwealth was attempting to elicit testimony from Menzie to establish that the Tyree marriage was one of discord. After some 160 pages of testimony from Menzie was mostly favorable to Tyree and the Tyree marriage, Menzie's entire testimony, some of it supportive of Tyree and some contrary to Tyree's penal interest, is clearly what most of us call hearsay.

The third entity to be examined is the credibility of the witnesses. When Mr. Menzie testified that Tyree had told him that Peters said, "People who keep books like that are going to get their throats cut," this was and is a relevant statement as to Menzie's and Peters' credibility. Menzie had testified truthfully without anything to profit from the decision. Peters had everything to gain from lying during his testimony and fabricating tales about Tyree. Peters not only lied in a matter relevant for the proceedings before Judge Killam, but he had done so in a matter that was severely inimical to Tyree's career as a Special Forces soldier.

Erik Aarhus's credibility falls under closer scrutiny and examination because he had already perjured himself during the Article 15 situation prior to the murder. Therefore, his statement to the CID is suspect at best. Then we have CID agent Burzynski, who stated that he had received authorization for the search from Colonel Rittgers even though the colonel held firm to his timeline of 6:10 p.m., an hour after the CID says they received permission and recovered the knife.

Eighteen years later, the Honorable James Killam III was interviewed about the events that unfolded during the probable cause hearing that he presided over. In that interview he recalled, "I was determined to hold the hearing as much of a fact-finding hearing as possible. One of the reasons was that since I had had some experience with the military, I knew witnesses in a case could be scattered to the four winds very shortly by an order of a commanding officer to another post. The next item is the preservation of the testimony. Testimony in a probable cause hearing is under oath, and so in order to preserve the testimony, I heard as many witnesses as possible to preserve the testimony for any later proceedings where it might be used by either side.

"It wasn't too long into the hearing that the government either was not proceeding along the most nearly apparent lines, and for whatever reason. The government was the laboring oar in the prosecution, has to have a theory of its case. Not too long into the proceedings, I had serious reservations about the course that the government was taking in the prosecution of the two defendants in this case. A few of the things led me to a belief contrary to what the government was presenting. That is the demeanor, presentation, behavior, almost studied lack of candor in the government's key witness in the case (Peters). The little things like a gaze at the ceiling which sometimes lasted twenty or thirty seconds before the answer to a question was delivered. Length of time which appeared to me to be putting the answer to the question into some scenario that was either pre-planned or was not actually the case. The government's key witness appeared to be not just a witness but rather before too long in the questioning, which gave me the impression he was the orchestrator of the proceedings. I felt that (his) questioning stopped before the real answers were coming out, and I did participate in the questioning of witnesses in this case"

If Judge Killam, an experienced lawyer and trial judge, could sense culpability in a witness, it raises the question as to why didn't the lawyers for Tyree and Aarhus monopolize on this during Peters' testimony? Instead, they treated Peters as if he were untouchable.

Judge Killam went on to further comment about the alleged murder weapon. "It stretches credibility. It stretches normal belief to find that a place that was subject to a search or daily inspection such as the barracks and bed of a soldier would hide the weapon and that weapon would be so carefully preserved for a two-week period. I can't imagine anyone believing that a perpetrator of a crime would save the weapon covered with evidence of the crime in two plastic bags and place it in the place that was easy to find. As far as I was concerned, that had to be planted."

Again, if a seasoned trial judge felt this way, why didn't the CID agents, Ayer Police Department, and the Massachusetts State Police not investigate further into the possibility of a setup?

Killam discussed two of the most troublesome witnesses during the hearing. "The business of presentation is a balancing of several factors. In this case, it appeared to me that the government was not offering an advantage to the key witness (Peters) but rather appeared to ignore his possible involvement in it. There was one assault after another on my ability to believe what was being presented in front of me. The assaults on my credibility came with such regularity during the course of the hearing. (Burzynski) was a witness in the case and happened to be one of the most reluctant, recalcitrant, obstructionist witnesses that I had ever faced in a court in my life. A worthless witness as far as I was concerned. He didn't want me to know anything."

Again, the CID and the key witness seemed to be withholding information and obstructing justice in this matter. It was so obvious that the presiding judge had an issue with it years later.

The last thing that Judge Killam said bothered him even before he drafted his decision was the manner in which Elaine Tyree was killed. "The victim, Elaine Tyree, was a large woman. Eric Aarhus was a small man. From the pictures and everything of the scene, from the body and so forth, it did not appear to me to be that type of relationship. There was also one more thing that bothered me almost to the end, before I drafted my decision. That was the cut throat. Now, one of the strange things about the pictures of the death scene was the fact that the throat was cut, and really if you want to say from ear to ear. Yet there was no blood in the vicinity of the cut throat. What looks to me as the cut throat in this case was cut to send a message after the blood had all gone to some other exit wound. My present belief is that the knife was wielded by other than the two people that are now in prison."

General Douglas MacArthur once said, "I am concerned for the security of our great nation; not so much because of any threat from without, but because of the insidious forces working from within." General MacArthur was warning the citizens of the United States against hidden or secret agendas that certain government departments or agencies might attempt to implement under the guise of national security and national interest. Government agencies such as the Central Intelligence Agency and the National Security Administration do not operate within the framework of the Constitution. These government groups work on the peripherals of the United States Constitution. They are in a gray area that influences foreign policy while never having to answer completely to the United States Senate, Congress, or the American public. These departments also have been known to use the military to help them accomplish their goals.

Most men and women join the military out of a sense of patriotism. They want to repay the United States in some small way by serving in the armed forces. When these young men and women are approached for certain covert operations, it never enters their mind that they might be participating in an unsanctioned and illegal government operation. They believe that they are keeping the United States safe from a threat.

**

The narcotics industry is the largest industry in the world, with $1 trillion annually in sales. During the mid-1970s, the Central Intelligence Agency became involved in drug trafficking on an industrial scale. Originally, it became involved to strongly adhere to anti-communist philosophy. Under this rule, the drug lords were aided and assisted in the production, transportation, and distribution of narcotics, and the proceeds were used to arm the resistance movements in these countries. In 1973, President Richard Nixon declared his War on Drugs.

During this time, heroin entered the United States from two pipelines: Southeast Asia, which was controlled by the CIA, and Turkey, from which it flowed through Marseilles under the control of the Corsican Crime Syndicate. The Turkish pipeline was effectively shut down because the Turkish government was a close ally of the United States and its War on Drugs This created a greater demand for heroin produced in the Golden Triangle of Southeast Asia, especially Burma.

In 1975, the CIA began Operation Watchtower. This was a covert mission that allowed drugs to be moved from Columbia to Panama and from there to the United States and other destinations. It began as a series of electronic beacons and transmitters. Once these towers were established with radio beacons, this allowed American drug planes to fly below Columbian radar from Bogota to Albrook Air Station in Panama. This was the perfect location to use since the airstrip and buildings were transferred to the Panama government on October 1, 1979. The idea was to create a safe corridor for planes to move guns south and cocaine north. The operation provided arms for right-wing El Salvador guerillas. Large quantities of drugs were not shipped for immediate sale but rather, prepositioned so they could be sold later when more money was needed to finance counter insurgency operations. This was what Bill Tyree claimed he had taken part in.

"I can't in good conscience allow the US government to destroy privacy, internet freedom, and basic liberties for people around the world with this massive surveillance machine they're secretly building." Edward Snowden

CHAPTER SIX

The Evidence Closes In

While the probable cause hearing was taking place, another mystery was about to unfold.

Massachusetts State trooper Roderick Hendrigan recalls, "On Wednesday, April 11, 1979, I was assigned to go to the Ayer District Courthouse to testify in a probable cause murder trial, Commonwealth vs. William Tyree and Eric Aarhus. The trial was sequestered; consequently, myself and other military and civilian witnesses weren't permitted in the courtroom. At approximately 10:30 a.m., Agents Paul Mason and Joseph Burzynski, United States Army Criminal Intelligence Division, and I were invited into the office of Ira Keizer, building superintendent of the Ayer Courthouse, for a cup of coffee. Keizer, an elderly man, started a conversation with the army officers about his experiences in the military. Keizer stated that his final years with the military he was attached to the Nike Missile Division with a top-secret clearance. He talked about his service in World War II, stating he was one of the first United States soldiers to enter Hiroshima after the atomic bomb was dropped. Keizer said he spent one year in an army hospital with radiation sickness. He said he had a lot of experience in demolitions and proceeded to tell several war stories.

"While talking with us, Keizer took a black, four-inch revolver from his desk, opened the cylinder, spun it, snapped it shut, placing the weapon in his trousers. During this discussion, courthouse matters were also discussed, namely security of the building and parking problems. Keizer brought up the subject of 'bugging,' as he called it. Keizer said he was an expert in bugging, that he once had been hired to bug a hotel room. He said police officials had approached him for assistance with bugs, naming Chief Barker of Littleton. He said on several occasions that he knew everything that was going on in the courthouse. Agent Burzynski specifically recalled Keizer saying that he bugged the entire courthouse. At approximately 11:00 a.m., Chief William Adamson of the Ayer Police came into Keizer's office and joined our discussion. At some point during this Discussion, Keizer, who was sitting at his desk in the corner of his office, swiveled his chair around and reaching behind him, turned on a small box. As Keizer did this, I heard a male voice coming from the device. I didn't recognize the voice at the time, but it did sound as if it were coming from the courtroom. Keizer said, 'That was the judge court is still in session.'

"After a short conversation Adamson, Mason, Burzynski, and I left Keizer's office. At this time, Adamson asked if I heard the voice. I said I had. He then asked if I know who it was I heard. I said only that Ira said it was the judge. Adamson said that he recognized the voice and it was Judge David Williams. Adamson and I had further conversation about Keizer. Adamson advised that Keizer had been seen in the courthouse at night with hand grenades attached to a bandolier and carrying a weapon.

"On Friday, April 13, 1979. I again was at the Ayer Court on the same case. At 1:00 p.m., Assistant District Attorney DeMichaelis, Chief Adamson, Trooper Keane, and I went to dinner. While eating, the subject of the courthouse being bugged came up. Chief Adamson and I related to DeMichaelis what happened two days prior in Ira Keizer's office. At this time, DeMichaelis stated that he was called into Judge David Williams' chambers to discuss the availability of a judge for the remaining portion of the probable cause hearing. When he went into the chambers, Judge Williams and Killam were present. Judge Williams told DeMichaelis that it wasn't advisable to talk in his chamber as he knew it was bugged. DeMichaelis suggested to me that on request of Judge Williams, I should institute an investigation. I advised Mr. DeMichaelis that I would have to clear any investigation with my supervisor, Detective George McGarity. At this time, Adamson said he would solve any problem by writing District Attorney Droney and requesting his office investigate.

"On Thursday, May 10, 1979, I was summoned to District Attorney Droney's office. Mr. Droney handed me a letter from Chief Adamson, Ayer Police, dated April 30, 1979. The letter explained the circumstances surrounding the events of April 11 and 13, 1979. District Attorney Droney, Assistant District Attorney Neylon, and I discussed the matter. I explained the event in Keizer's office as I recalled. At that time, I was instructed by Mr. Droney to institute an investigation into the matter, this case to be handled in. Mr. Droney also instructed that Mr. Richard Barry, First Security Company Boston, be called as consultant as an expert in electronic surveillance. Mr. Barry was contacted and a meeting with him, Neylon, McGarity, and I was set up for Wednesday, May 16, 1979. At the meeting, Barry was apprised of the situation and he suggested that he would have his electronics expert as well as a team of men and equipment capable of sweeping the court for bugging devices. The decision as to access into the court was discussed. However, final decision on that was to come from the district attorney.

"On May 24, 1979, I wrote an affidavit for a search warrant for the Ayer District Courts. Myself and Assistance District Attorneys Neylon and Agnes took the affidavit to the second session of the superior court to Judge Tambarello. The judge, after careful examination of the affidavit, issued a search warrant naming electronic surveillance equipment as that which was to be seized.

"Same date at approximately 4:00 p.m., McGarity, I, and officers from the State Police Middlesex District Attorney's office, Assistant District Attorneys Neylon and Agnes, met with Mr. Richard G. Barry and his team of electronics people at the court. The team was headed by Marc Nezer, electronic expert, John P. Winslow, photographer, Jeff Shorter, alarm, and Bruce Dean, Kenneth Dorch, Paul Nalezienski, and Steve Goodhue. We immediately entered the court, at which time I went directly to the office of Ira Keizer, the building superintendent. I entered his office accompanied by Mr. Richard Barry. I displayed my badge, advised him who I was, also advising him I was in possession of a search warrant for bugging devices. At this time, Keizer went from his desk to a file cabinet in the corner of the room. He took a small, black purse from the cabinet and stated, 'It's pay day. You don't mind if I take my purse?'

"At this time, Mr. Barry requested everything be left alone as we had a warrant. I advised Keizer the warrant was being shown to Judge Williams, that I would get it and return to the office. I went to the first floor, obtained the warrant from Assistant District Attorney Neylon, and returned to Keizer's office, where he and Barry were waiting. Keizer viewed the warrant at this time, and the black purse was taken from his coat pocket. The purse was opened and I observed a small, black microphone. Garry advised he felt the item was a small, wireless transmitter. At this time, Cpl. Latham and I advised Mr. Keizer of his rights under Miranda, and card was signed by Keizer at that time.

Subsequently, a search was made of Keizer's office, which revealed a substantial amount of bugging paraphernalia; some of the more notable pieces are a miniature remote control microphone, two AM-FM radios, which were tuned to act as receivers for the miniature transmitters. There were two telephone boxes with attached hookups for telephone taping and a desk calendar with a hidden microphone. There are numerous other devices which were seized from Keizer's office.

"Keizer made several statements to me and other State Police officers during the course of this search. Keizer stated that he expected something like this to happen because he had been telling people for some time, he bugged the building. When the desk calendar was discovered to have a microphone in it, he admitted to making it. He also admitted to making a telephone box containing a hook-up for a telephone tape. He stated a girl made his other telephone box. He stated to me that he had the capability to go into any office in the court. He stated all he would do was drop the bug in the room at night after everyone had left, then retrieve it the next night. While sitting in the second-floor courtroom, Keizer expressed an interest in telling myself, Cpl. Latham, and Mr. Barry why he had to protect Judge David Williams.

"Keizer was again advised of his rights in the presence of Latham and Barry. Keizer stated that several years ago, he and Judge Williams were in Texas attending a convention of the National Disabled American Veterans Organization, at which the judge was going to be named to a high post. Keizer and Williams went across the border into Mexico. He stated at this time pornography was illegal, and Judge Williams was heavy into it. He said the judge bought several pornographic articles while in Mexico, and as they were returning to this county were stopped by the border patrol. The pornography was in plain view in the front seat. When asked whose it was Keizer lied and said it was his. Keizer felt he had less to lose than the judge. Keizer was arrested; each spent the night in a motel. The next day, Keizer went to court, was fined and turned over to the United States Army authorities as he was in the military at that time. This was the reason Keizer felt he had to protect Williams.

"Keizer felt that it was his function as building superintendent to be in charge of security for the building and stated that he had installed some electric locks in various locations in the building. He felt one of his basic functions was to protect the judge. For this reason, he said he would drop a wireless microphone down outside the window of the judges' lobby, thus being able to hear conversation within the lobby. He did say at this time that when I was in his office, I was listening to a conversation in the judges' lobby, not in the courtroom. Keizer defied the team sweeping the courthouse to find any bugs. He stated they didn't have the correct equipment and they didn't know where to look. He implied he knew more about bugging than our electronics expert.

"Det. McGarity and I asked Mr. Keizer if we could have his permission to search his camper van which was parked in the lot to the rear of the court. Keizer granted permission to enter the van, but then stated he had a young lady in the van and requested we leave her alone McGarity and I accompanied Keizer to his van. Upon entering a young lady, Ann Norris, was lying down on the bed. The camper was searched by the above officers with negative results.

"At this time, we continued our search in the main court, judges lobby, with the first security electronics team. Mr. Nezer finished Judge David Williams' lobby with negative results. While sweeping Judge Arthur Williams' lobby, Nezer found a small diode in the telephone, which he believed was a hot mic. Nezer described this hot mic as having capability of transmitting a voice to a receiver, whether the phone was in use or the receiver on the hook. As a result of finding this hot mic, Nezer again re-checked the adjoining judges' lobbies. At this time, Nezer found similar diodes in other lobby phones.

"I accompanied Nezer to the basement of the courthouse, where we discovered two wires hanging from the ceiling. The wires were traced through the ceiling up the elevator shaft, through the first-floor ceiling, ending in the PA system in the foyer of the courthouse. Later that evening, I talked with Mr. Alf Neilson, courthouse employee, who stated he ran the wires in order to allow employees to hear the PA system in the basement. Nezer questioned this wiring, as Neilson said it was done eight years prior, but the wire was found in Keizer's office. Nezer did say that the wires would allow the PA to be heard in the basement. At this time, the search of the court was concluded at approximately 4:30 a.m. The search netted sixty-six pieces of electronic surveillance equipment and numerous tapes.

On May 25, 1979, I wrote a second affidavit for a search warrant. Second warrant issued by Judge Tambarello. This affidavit was the result of Nezer requesting assistance from the telephone company regarding the diode found in several court phones. Telephone company repairmen were also summoned by court employees as phones were malfunctioning the morning of May 25, 1979. Upon arrival, members of the telephone company, First Security, were present at the court. They are the electronic surveillance team for the Massachusetts State Police. Telephone repairmen checked the diode thought to be a hot mic, and said it was a telephone company-installed dial restrictor. The problem with the court phones was that the main court phone was attached to the pay phone. The result was inability to call out from the court phones. Nezer believed this wiring mistake to be made after we left the night prior as phones were working properly at that time.

"At this time, Judge David Williams requested we take any weapons that were in Keizer's office out of the court for the security of the court. Judge Williams gave me a written order to that effect. I went to Keizer's office and seized a .41 caliber Smith and Wesson revolver and a Mauser semi-automatic pistol. Also seized was a hand grenade, checked and made safe. Examination of the weapons revealed the serial numbers on the revolver were obliterated. The weapons were taken to the State Police Ballistics Laboratory for examination."

Mr. Keizer was taken into custody and officially charged with the illegal surveillance of the First District Courthouse of Northern Middlesex County. The longest probable cause hearing in the history of the Massachusetts judiciary, which lasted twelve-and one-half days, had been illegally bugged.

"In the councils of government, we must guard against the acquisition of unwarranted influence, whether sought or unsought, by the military-industrial complex. The potential for the disastrous rise of misplaced power exists, and will persist." President Dwight D. Eisenhower

CHAPTER SEVEN

Big Brother Was Listening

When the bugging of the courthouse was discovered, it was never made known to Judge Killam III or the attorneys until after the probable cause hearing. Once Bill and his attorney discovered the illegal bugging of the courthouse, they immediately raised the issue of Coplon v. United States 191 F.2d 749, 757-758 (D.C. 1951) "… If a citizen is under surveillance, it must end when the citizen is indicted…"

Even though Bill clearly demonstrated that his right to effective assistance of counsel had been denied by the failure of the prosecution team to either stop the surveillance or stop the probable cause hearing, the Massachusetts court rejected his petition. If this was not bad enough, the Massachusetts Supreme Judicial Court handed down a ruling on the lower court. They declared that Earl Michael Peters was not to be arrested for the murder of Elaine Tyree. Secondly, no court or law enforcement agency would be allowed to arrest anyone in connection with this case. What they effectively did was throw out the statutory mandates directing the arrest if probable cause exists, so effectively that no one could be arrested in this case without prior SJC approval.

In recent years, a letter has surfaced dated December 5, 1979, from John Droney to Colonel Cutolo. The letter is as follows:

Dear Colonel Cutolo,

Due to the nature of this letter, it is being delivered to you in person by Lt. Dwyer.

This letter is to inform you that I have concluded my part of our arrangement. SP4 Earl Michael Peters will not be arrested as a result of the order of Judge Killam. You may rest assured that SP4 Peters will not be subjected to any judicial review that pertains to the Elaine Tyree homicide. My office views SP4 Peters as the main witness to the tragic events that culminated in the murder of Elaine Tyree.

As in regards to your part of our arrangement, I would ask that you provide Lt. Dwyer with all audio-visual matter you collected concerning me. In specific, I would like the material relating to Mr. Cook and his escape from the East Cambridge Jail, not to mention the material relating to my alternative lifestyle. My constituents have narrow and conventional views, and therefore, my homosexuality is better left unknown.

Incidentally, I recommend the surveillance material collected at the Tyree residence on January 30, 1979, if you have not already done so.

In closing, I would add that you may contact me at any time. I am at your disposal.

John Droney, District Attorney

The letter was written on Droney's office letterhead. However, no attempts to authenticate the letter have been made since its discovery. With that being said, the letter, if authentic, validates what Bill claimed he heard while on a surveillance team outside of Droney's home and gives a reason for the unusual outcome of the probable cause hearing and trial.

While Bill was in the Billerica House of Correction awaiting trial, an odd occurrence took place. He recalls, "I was told that I would be put in a jail cell as close to the guards' desk as possible to assure I didn't do anything else at this point. I picked up what things that belonged to me that they felt weren't harmful or could be used to hurt others with, and went to unit I-3. Well, I was about to watch television when Brian Brett, who was in L-23, came to the cell door to talk to me, because no one believed what had happened because I was a runner out from 7:30 a.m. to 5:30 p.m. at night.

While we were talking, I opened a Coke. I started to drink it and had about ten sips the whole time Brian was talking to me. It hit me like a brick that something was in the Coke. At first, I couldn't tell what it was, then Brian took it and said it smelled like ammonia or cleaning solvent. The guards came to the cell and took me to the hospital. I was throwing up all the time. Well, they said at the hospital that nothing was in me, or traces of anything. I came back to Billerica and went into my cell and lay down, at which point I found the suicide note. I called the guard over and gave him the note, then in a few minutes the guard came back and took me to the infirmary. I was told to strip and forced to sleep on the floor on a mattress. That night, Jim Kee, a fellow inmate, asked me why I didn't finish the can of Coke I had started on. I told him it didn't taste right and he dumped it out, and there was a whole bunch of yellow stuff on the bottom. We both smelled it and came to the conclusion that it could be Valiums. I found out that there was twenty-five of them crushed and put into the can, but the guy that did it thought he was getting another guy."

Another strange letter was mailed to Tyree while he was incarcerated at the Billerica House of Correction. The envelope it came in was a standard Department of the Army envelope and the return address was "AEZD-JA-DG-AF

Fort Devens Ma." In the envelope was a four-page typed letter. It was addressed "To whom it may concern" and had Earl Michaels Peters' signature at the top of the page. The format of the letter began as a statement and declaration of his last will and dying declaration.

The letter stated, "On January 30,1979, at 11:30 a.m., myself and two other guys that work for Jimmy entered Bill Tyree's apartment on Washington Street in Ayer, looking for a set of books that Elaine Tyree was keeping. In these books were times, dates, and places of certain illegal activities that I and others in and around Fort Devens were involved in. The day that she was killed, Erik Y. Aarhus was driving the car we used to go to the Tyree apartment, and he never entered the apartment. I didn't mean to kill Elaine. It was an accident. I told this to Bill the night he was arrested. She threatened to tell Bill I was in the apartment when he came home and he would have known why I was there."

The letter continued, "I didn't tell him who really killed her until just a few minutes before they were supposed to come get Aarhus. See, he told me and Testagrossa that he was going to set Aarhus up, and I decided to set both of them up and get away with murder. She came in the door of the apartment. As she turned to shut the door, I stabbed her in the left arm, that is why there is blood on the outside of the door and on the floor. As soon as I stabbed her, Jimmy's people grabbed her and threw her across the room, she knocked over a table and knocked all of the stuff on it to the floor. They then threw her back across the couch. In the process I think I stabbed her in the chest once. She screamed, like I had stabbed her in the heart. But she started to get up and that is when they held her down and I finished her off. She told me she hid the books outside next to the house. They left by way of the door and I left through the window. When I was leaving there was someone knocking at the door."

The letter continued on about things that Peters had allegedly done throughout his life with friends and family, and his alleged remorse for the crime. Each page of the letter is initialed "EMP" and signed on the first page and the third. This type of initialing is similar to CID practices. The letter has never been authenticated, although the signature appears to be similar to known samples of Peters' signature.

Another alleged Peters confession letter surfaced while Bill was still in the Billerica House of Correction. It contained similar content as the one that was mailed to Bill. However, the circumstances of this letter were much more mysterious.

An inmate, Michael Sullivan, was also incarcerated at the house of corrections at this time. In his 1987 affidavit he states, "During my incarceration in the jail portion of the house of corrections, I came to know an inmate trustee/ runner named James Young. James Young was a soldier stationed at Fort Devens when he was arrested in 1979. I heard of William Tyree, but state under oath that at no time did I know him as a friend and don't remember speaking to him at any time. What I vaguely recall of the crime James Young was arrested for, I believe that Young told me he was arrested for several things, but the crime I believe he told me of involved the breaking and entering of the Department of Public Works garage on the John Fitch Highway in Fitchburg-Leominster, Massachusetts. After becoming friendly with Young in late 1979, November or December, he spoke to me about William Tyree. Young stated that he had typed a three-page letter and threw it into William Tyree's cell, while Tyree had been in the isolation unit of the house of corrections. Young said, as near as I can recall, that he was told to do it by a screw, but did not name the officer. 'Screw' is a slang term for correctional officer. Young also said that Tyree knew the guy that 'fucked him' on a drug transaction, and the letter evened the score as far as he was concerned."

These mysterious letters only add to the speculation and conspiracy theories surrounding this case.

Erik Aarhus was tried first. Bill and his lawyer were never notified when the trial was begun. Aarhus had been offered a plea agreement from the State of Massachusetts. The offer was contingent on him testifying against Bill. He refused the offer and went to trial. During the probable cause hearing and the ensuing trial, Aarhus was housed in the Charles Street Jail in Boston, Massachusetts, while Bill was incarcerated in the Billerica House of Correction. This was to keep them segregated due to their charges.

Bill Tyree's trial started on Thursday, February 7, 1980. The first motion addressed was the prepayment of a witness's air fare, which the court allowed. The next three motions that attorney Bradley brought up were for continuance, change of venue, and sequestration of jury. Bradley made the argument for a change of venue based on the local newspaper coverage of Aarhus's trial and the alleged allegations made against his client, William Tyree.

Bradley stated, "Read the newspapers over the past several months, several weeks certainly. There are... and in particular in the *Lowell Sun* had a report, it has a rather large circulation, of course, throughout the entire northern part of this county. There are special editions that are distributed throughout the county to the towns of Concord, Acton, Lexington, and Ayer. And all the articles I have read, there has been specific reference to the defendant, Aarhus. In many of these articles appears the title 'Tyree' in rather large letters and the name 'Aarhus' and many of them specifically refer to the defendant, Aarhus, saying, 'Well, Tyree hired me, paid me, or something, had something to do with the killing of Elaine Tyree.' The timing here seems to be bad in that we have—you have—just sent out a jury in the Aarhus case.

"Those jurors are sitting in this Commonwealth now, in Middlesex County, who have already received notice of future attendance here as jurors. I suppose they are much more aware of what is reported in the newspaper as court proceedings are concerned now. And I think that has maybe worked to the detriment of the defendant, Tyree. I think that at this time, he would not be able to get a fair trial. I think it would be extremely difficult, if not impossible, at this time to empanel a jury that has not heard of, read of this. Now you have the jury in the Aarhus case already back with vital questions. It seems within the courtroom while we have a jury deliberating on the fate of one co-defendant, we are going to try and pick another jury and put them to trial in the same crime. I think that that is dangerous as far as a fair trial is concerned. It seems to me that it is very dangerous, and I am talking now as I know I suggested to you, off the top of my head, but I have had time to consider this and I wonder whether or not any great harm would be done by continuing this until the first week of March, first Monday of March, whenever you want to do it and go forward at that time.

"I am aware that the Commonwealth has some concern as far as the witnesses, but I do think that our prime concern should be a fair trial, that we want to give the defendant a fair and expedient trial. Cost should not stand in our way. And I feel that the publicity has been detrimental to the defendant."

In the end, the motion was denied and Bradley objected, which was noted on the record.

Three days later, the jury had been selected and the trial was set to get underway. The Honorable Judge Young was presiding. The initial proceedings began as follows:

The court: We will start now. I just hope to get through so that we can start with the jury. The first matter to handle is the question of sequestration of witnesses. Upon reflection, I have decided that Agent Mason, in addition to Chief Adamson, may be present in the courtroom during such period of time any military witness is testifying, but at no other time. Chief Adamson is exempted from sequestration and may be present throughout the trial. You have instructed all of these people, Mr. McCormick, the witnesses that you will call, and Mr. Bradley, the witnesses you will call, with respect to the sequestration?

Mr. Bradley: Yes, Judge. There is a possibility, Your Honor, a mere possibility I may call Mrs. Tyree, the defendant's mother. She is in the room. I ask she be allowed to stay here.

The court: Mr. McCormick?

Mr. McCormick: Well, if Your Honor please, I have no problem with that, although I would point out to the Court that I have a similar situation in which Elaine Tyree's mother is involved relative to her being present during the course of the trial. I intend to call her, no question about that. I would ask if the Court allows Mrs. Tyree to remain in the courtroom, then I would ask the Court to allow Mrs. Hebb to remain, the victim's mother, to remain in the room.

The court: Mrs. Tyree is excused. I think members of the family ought to be present. We will say that she may be present throughout the trial. She understood my instructions not to discuss the case with anyone else who will be a witness. We will defer on the question of Mrs. Hebb. She may have an interest, but she is not a party. I am going to hold that. You will let me know when she arrives.

Mr. McCormick: Fine, Your Honor.

The court: You plan to call her?

Mr. McCormick: As a witness, yes, Your Honor, she is going to be a witness."

It seems odd that after Ayer Police Chief William Adamson, who was warned twice by Judge Killam about possible witness tampering, was allowed to be in the courtroom unsequestered. Either Judge Young didn't know about the warning or didn't feel it was important.

Assistant District Attorney McCormick began his opening statement. "Madam Forelady, ladies and gentlemen of the jury, now it becomes my function to sort of lay a roadmap out, if you will, of where this case will go. As His Honor has said, whatever I say at any juncture during the course of this trial is not evidence. What I am saying now is just to be used as a guide, sort of a guidepost as to where the Commonwealth will be going. Evidence will come again from the witness stand, through the witnesses and exhibits that are presented. The Commonwealth will produce evidence in this case to show beyond a reasonable doubt that William Tyree did, in fact, have his wife killed, murdered. The evidence will be basically or the theory, I should say, will be that William Tyree did not, in fact, himself kill Elaine Tyree. The evidence will show that at a certain time, William Tyree got someone else, Erik Aarhus, to kill his wife. The evidence will open up on January 30, 1979.

"You will hear from the next-door neighbor, Mrs. Eliades. She was in her apartment, and she will testify that she lives in Apartment 3. She made certain observations out her kitchen window relative to this defendant, what he was doing. She will tell you what she saw. She will tell you that a short time later she heard a scream, a blood-curdling -scream from the next apartment, Apartment 1. She will tell you what she did. The first thing she did, she picked up the telephone and called the police, before she did anything, because of that scream. She will then tell you that she went out, went by door Number 1, and she rapped on the door. 'Elaine, Elaine are you there? Are you all right?' There was no response. She then went up to the platform at the top of the stairs where the main door is and she will tell you how she held the door open and she stood there and looked out, waiting for the police to arrive. She will tell you that she saw the officer pull in, straight in front of the other apartment and then pull over and park at the beginning of that macadam pathway into 104 1/2. She will tell you how the officer came up, there was a conversation. They went down to the door. She will tell you what the officer did relative to knocking on the door and trying to get some response out of that apartment.

"You will hear from the officer that after arriving at the door and getting no response, he went outside to make a radio communication. That a short time thereafter, the chief of police, William Adamson, arrived. The officer will tell you that when he went into the apartment building, he didn't see any screen on the ground. When he came out to make his call, there was a screen on the ground and the bedroom window, the window looking out to the parking lot was open and there was no screen on it. The officer will tell you he went over, after looking in the window, again trying to get some response from who was in there. 'Can I help you? I'm a police officer.' The officer will tell you that he and the chief went down and again tried to gain entry to that apartment, knocking on the door, trying the doorknob.

"You will hear evidence that the landlord, a Mr. Gardner, was summoned with a key. When he arrived, he opened the door and stepped back. You will hear evidence that as the chief went into that apartment, the body of Elaine Tyree was lying on the floor, on the carpet right near the linoleum, in the kitchen. She was lying on her back with her face up in the air, with blood on her face and her throat cut. You will hear testimony from Lieutenant Decott as to what he observed in that apartment shortly after 12:00 p.m. on January 30, 1979.

"You will see pictures of how that lady was lying there when they went in. You will hear evidence that a short time later a telephone call was received at the apartment and at that time it was Billy Tyree. And that he was told to come immediately. You will hear evidence relative to the observations that the officers made relative to Billy Tyree.

"There will be evidence that just outside the main gate at Fort Devens near the Devens Shopping Plaza, Billy Tyree was pulled over by one of the officers and taken down to the police station. You will hear evidence that he went into the conference room and there was a conference in the conference room. You will hear evidence as to what observations the officer made of Bill Tyree that afternoon. You will hear evidence as to what happened. You will hear evidence as to what Bill Tyree said that afternoon and also about what he did, what he said about where he was precisely at 12:15 p.m. You will hear evidence that later on, they went back to the apartment with Bill Tyree so that he could get some clothes. You will hear evidence that the following day, Bill Tyree was questioned further. You will hear what he had to say relative to what he had to say the earlier day, the day before the 30th. This is on the 31st, in the evening at the CID building at Devens. He was brought in. He sat down and he answered some questions about why he was back to the house twice that morning, once at 11:20 a.m. to bring a baby seat back and once at five minutes of twelve to bring his wife back.

"You will hear evidence that Erik Aarhus, a soldier in the Special Forces at Fort Devens, was a soldier with Bill Tyree. You will hear evidence that the investigation went on. You will hear testimony of the officers relative to their observations of Bill Tyree and his reactions as to his wife's death. You will hear how there was a funeral detail and how they traveled to Cumberland, Maryland to bury Elaine Tyree. You will hear evidence that she was twenty-two years of age, that she had a two-month-old daughter, Dawn. You will hear, ladies and gentlemen, evidence relative to what happened down in Cumberland, Maryland when Bill Tyree was down there to bury his wife. You will hear about what happened at the Holiday Inn down there.

"There will be evidence presented by the Commonwealth with reference to two young ladies who were in the service, to which Bill Tyree made advances to. You will hear them testify to what those advances were. You will hear testimony relative to the atmosphere down at this hotel, the celebration. You will hear testimony from other soldiers relative to what Bill Tyree was like the next day, the 31st, the next day, February 1st.

"You will hear from Dennis Testagrossa, a soldier in the United States Army, about how Tyree treated him, bought him dinner and bought him drinks. You will hear what happened down in Cumberland, Maryland relative to the incident in Bill Tyree's motel room. You will hear from the officer that responded to a trouble call and he will describe what he observed in relation to what Bill Tyree told him relative to the room being locked up and Bill Tyree having someone in the room, supposedly hurting him. You will hear evidence relative to Mr. Tyree going to the Walter Reed Army Hospital shortly after this, but again, these witnesses will give you their observations of Bill Tyree. You will hear evidence relative to his coming back to Fort Devens.

"The evidence will show that on February 9, Bill Tyree returned to the base. He had a conversation with the post commander, Colonel Rittgers, relative to what had been transpiring. You will hear evidence relative to February 12, the police had another conversation with Bill Tyree. You will hear evidence that on that day, the police began to bring more pressure and that the interview went on at length, about inconsistencies and about what he had said earlier and what he was saying now.

"You will hear evidence how the police learned certain things as they went along, that Erik Aarhus had been at the house on the evening of January 29,, the night before the killing. You will hear evidence that he was invited over there by William Tyree to discuss some matters and that when Erik Aarhus went to the apartment, Mr. Tyree was at the movie theater watching a movie. You will hear evidence that after the interview on February 12, 1979, that William Tyree, the following day, February 13, brought, opened the case. William Tyree contacted Chief William Adamson that afternoon. He had been telling the police, and you will hear evidence to this effect, that it was one of two people, either Erik Aarhus or a chap by the name of Rio. On February 13, 1979, William Tyree called Chief Adamson and he told Chief Adamson that day that Erik Aarhus had the murder weapon, a knife, a Buck knife. You will hear evidence at the Devens Shopping Plaza, the one that you were parked at having your coffee and donuts yesterday, that the police staked out that area so that Bill Tyree, this man here, could lure Erik Aarhus off the base with the murder weapon, because you will hear evidence that Bill Tyree told Erik Aarhus he was glad that he had killed his wife, and that now he wanted the murder weapon back. Bill Tyree talked to Erik Aarhus: 'I want the murder weapon back.' You will hear evidence to that effect. You will hear evidence that Bill Tyree subsequently offered $1,000 and then $5,000 to get Erik Aarhus to bring the murder weapon back. You will hear evidence that while the police were parked there at that shopping plaza, nothing happened. They received a call from Bill Tyree: 'I can't get Aarhus off the base.' You will hear evidence from the witnesses the Commonwealth will present that at that time, the early evening hours of February 13, they left the Devens Shopping Plaza and they traveled directly to the CID building, which is located on Post at Fort Devens.

"At that time, after the officers entered the CID building, you will hear evidence that right behind them, maybe a minute or two, Bill Tyree came in. You will hear evidence that he came in and he told the police officers, 'I just saw the knife. It's in a plastic bag and it's down in Aarhus's room.' You will hear evidence that Aarhus lived in Room 139 at the barracks. You will hear evidence to describe that room being the last room down on the right-hand side from the armor room. Erik Aarhus's room.

"You will hear testimony that when Bill Tyree came into the CID building and he told the police that he had certain things, that as a result of what William Tyree told the officials that night, they went down to Erik Aarhus's room. And when they went down there, you will hear evidence that underneath the pillow, just as Bill Tyree told them, was the murder weapon wrapped up in a plastic bag. You will hear evidence that that murder weapon still had blood on it. You will hear evidence from the chemist that that blood is Type B- blood and you will hear evidence that Elaine Tyree had Type B- blood.

"You will hear evidence that at the time Bill Tyree was in the conference room at the CID building, he was writing out a statement relative to the finding of the knife and the reason why Erik Aarhus killed his wife. You will hear further evidence in this case from other soldiers—Michael Peters, another soldier assigned to the Green Berets at Fort Devens.

"You will hear Mr. Peters testify that before this, he was a friend of William Tyree and that sometime in late 1978, Mr. Tyree approached him and asked him if he could kill his wife, if Peters could take and hit a moving target at fifty-five miles an hour from a bridge abutment. You will hear evidence that this wasn't the only time. Peters will testify that after that, he talked again about getting rid of his wife, maybe driving the four-wheel vehicle off the side of a mountain. There will be more testimony relative to Peters and Bill Tyree engaging somebody else to kill his wife.

"You will hear testimony from some of the witnesses, some of the people that lived in that apartment building. You will hear testimony relative to what the relationship was that Bill Tyree and his wife had. You will hear testimony that he left his wife alone. You will hear further testimony that subsequent to the baby being born in November, Bill Tyree purchased a $20,000 life insurance policy. You will hear further testimony that in January of 1979, a week or weeks before the actual killing, that Bill Tyree went and bought another $20,000 insurance policy on his wife. You will hear testimony from Mr. Peters that the Sunday before the killing, which would be January 28, he observed Mr. Tyree parked outside the front door of that barracks of the 10th Special Forces where you were yesterday, in his pick-up truck with Erik Aarhus.

"You will hear testimony that Earl Michael Peters was on the second floor looking out a window, and he had a conversation with Mr. Tyree about what Mr. Tyree was doing. You will hear what Mr. Tyree had to say regarding what he was doing with Erik Aarhus. Just negotiating. The Commonwealth will show beyond a reasonable doubt that Erik Aarhus killed Elaine Tyree on January 30, 1979. First, it will show beyond a reasonable doubt that William Tyree participated in that killing, either in concert with Erik Aarhus at the time or as an accessory before the fact. The Commonwealth will prove each and every element in the indictment that you people will decide on beyond a reasonable doubt that William Tyree did, in fact, do what he is charged with doing. Thank you very much, ladies and gentlemen."

Judge Young then proceeded to ask Mr. Bradley if he would like to make an opening statement, to which he replied, "No, Your Honor. No, I think I will wait till the conclusion of the Commonwealths case."

After a brief recess, the trial resumed and the Commonwealth's first witness, Mrs. Eliades was called to the stand. She testified to hearing Elaine's scream and calling the Ayer Police. She gave the same testimony that she had given in the probable cause hearing.

The next witness was Ayer Police officer Walter Decott. He was questioned extensively about the open window at the apartment at 104 ½ Washington Street. His testimony is as follows:

Decott: I looked at the building, looked up at the building. Looked at the windows.

ADA McCormick: Did you notice anything?

Decott: Yes, sir. I noticed a window on the west side of the building where there wasn't any screen on the window. And I observed the bottom portion of that, the glass portion of the window being open and the drapery curtain kind of blowing in the wind.

ADA McCormick: Westerly may not mean a lot to some of us. So could you tell us in relationship to the parking lot where that window was?

Decott: It would be on the parking lot side of the building as you pulled in the parking lot, before the walkway. It would be that side of the building as you would look at it.

ADA McCormick: Was that the first window on the first floor?

Decott: Yes, sir.

ADA McCormick: After you made your observations of that window, that the window was open, did you do something?

Decott: Yes, sir.

ADA McCormick: What did you do, sir?

Decott: Went over to the window and looked inside.

ADA McCormick: Would you tell us what you observed?

Decott: The room, untidy room. Looked like a full-sized bed on the right-hand side as you looked in. On the left-hand side running parallel to the wall was a dresser and I don't remember just where, but I remember observing a crib in that area, a child's crib in the room, also.

This was the only part of Decott's testimony that was more detailed than his previous testimony at the probable cause hearing.

The next witness was Lieutenant Arthur Boisseau of the Ayer Police Department. He testified about what he saw when he entered the apartment. When questioned about the couch, he stated, "That is a couch that opens up into a bed."

McCormick: Will you describe to the Court and the members of the jury, how it opens up into a bed?

Boisseau: The back to the couch will lie flat. The back and the seating area is the bed space.

McCormick: It's not one of those pull-out couches, is it?

Boisseau: No, the bottom seating area of the couch can be lifted for a storage space in the frame of the couch itself.

On the fifth day of the trial, Massachusetts State Police officer Roderick Hendrigan testified about Bill's whereabouts the morning of the murder. "He stated at approximately 5:30 a.m. in the morning he left with his wife, his daughter. He took his daughter to the babysitter; he dropped his wife off at the US Army garrison where she worked. He said he returned home to the apartment.

"At 7:00 a.m., he went back to the base, picked up his wife, and returned home. At 8:00, he again returned to the base. This time he drove a neighbor, Jane Gibson, to the bus and returned to the base. At 9:40 a.m., he said he went to the military traffic court. He left there at 11:00 a.m. in the morning. At 11:10 a.m., he said he went over to the TDA maintenance to pick up some typewriters, which he put in the back of his pick-up truck.

"He said that approximately 11:30 a.m., he called his wife to tell her to remember the baby's doctor's appointment, which was that afternoon at 2:00 p.m. He said that between 11:45 a.m. and 11:50 a.m., he picked up his wife where she worked and started home. They stopped at a grocery store and picked up some things for dinner. They went back to the apartment. He told her he wasn't going to go in, but check the mail. She got out of the car to go out and check the mail. He looked at his watch and it was 12:05 p.m. He told me that he had to get the typewriters back or the first sergeant was going to have his ass, so he tooted the horn twice and drove back to the detachment. He said he arrived back there around 12:15 p.m. I asked how he knew the time. He said, well, Lieutenant Klein had asked him what time it was and he looked at his watch. I said, 'Well, how do you know it was 12:05 p.m. in the parking lot of your apartment?' He said, 'My wife gave me a watch for Christmas and I'm in the habit of looking at it.' He said that at 12:15 p.m., he unloaded the typewriters. He was assisted by Spec 5 Beecham."

After almost five days of testimony, the Commonwealth produced no evidence that Bill was in any way implicated, never mind guilty of having his wife killed.

On cross examination, Mr. Bradley asked Officer Hendrigan about what evidence was taken from the Tyree apartment. When he questioned him about the diaries, Hendrigan testified to the following:

Bradley: Were there any small books at the Tyree apartment under the television set?

Hendrigan: I'm not sure if they were under the television set.

Bradley: You're not sure if they were under the television, but there were books of that nature?

Mr. McCormick: Objection.

Hendrigan: Yes, sir.

The court: The objection is overruled. The answer may stand.

Bradley: What were these books?

Hendrigan: Would you restate the question, sir?

Bradley: They were small books, diary-type books in that apartment? Who took them?

Mr. McCormick: Objection to the question, if Your Honor please.

The court: Sustained, in that form.

Bradley: You saw some small, diary-type books in that apartment?

Mr. McCormick: Objection.

The court: Overruled.

Hendrigan: No.

Bradley: A moment ago, Mr. Witness, you said there were books, not under the television set, small diary-type books. Where were they?

MR. McCormick: Objection.

The court: Sustained. Let's find out what he saw.

Bradley: All right. May I? A moment ago, Mr. Witness, I asked you if you saw under the television set on the stand some small diary-type books. Your answer was they were not under the television set? My question is—

Mr. McCormick: Objection.

The court: Let him put his question, Mr. McCormick.

Bradley: My question is: Where were they?

Mr. McCormick: Objection, Your Honor.

The court: Sustained.

Mr. McCormick: Thank you, Your Honor.

Bradley: May I approach the bench, Your Honor?

The court: You may.

The conference at the bench went like this:

Bradley: He said they were small, diary-type. He responded to my question that they were. May we have it read back, please?

The court: Certainly.

Bradley: Could I have the last question read?

The court: Yes. (The question is read.)

Bradley: Can you answer that?

Hendrigan: I don't believe that was my answer, sir.

Bradley: You don't believe that is your answer?

Hendrigan: No, sir.

Bradley: What do you think your answer was?

Mr. McCormick: Objection.

The court: Sustained.

Bradley: Did you hear the question just read back to you?

Hendrigan: Yes, sir.

Bradley: You did not make that response?

Hendrigan: You asked, when that was read back, what is your response to my response to the prior question?

Bradley: Let's try it again. Do you know where the television set was in the room?

Hendrigan: Yes, sir.

Bradley: The television set was on the stand?

Hendrigan: Correct.

Bradley: I asked you whether or not on that stand underneath the television set you saw some diary-type books and your response to me was, "Not under there."

Mr. McCormick: Objection.

Bradley: Or whether or not on that—

Mr. McCormick: Objection.

The court: Just a moment, let him finish the question.

Bradley: I'm rephrasing it the best I can. I then asked you where they were. All right. Where they were?

The court: You may have that question, but the witness need not answer yes or no. You may have it and he may respond if he does not understand the question.

Hendrigan: I don't believe I ever said that they were not under the television there.

Bradley: Where were they?

Hendrigan: My answer was, "I'm not sure."

Bradley: Were they in that apartment?

Hendrigan: Yes, sir.

Bradley: You took them?

Hendrigan: No, sir.

Bradley: Who took them?

Hendrigan: One of the investigators.

Bradley: Who?

Hendrigan: I'm sorry, I can't tell you now, sir.

Bradley: Who was in charge of this?

Hendrigan: Detective Lieutenant Jack Dwyer of the Massachusetts State Police.

Bradley: Did he have them?

Hendrigan: I'm sure he saw them, yes, sir.

Bradley You're sure what?

Hendrigan: I'm sure I saw them, yes, sir.

Bradley: But you don't know what happened to them?

Hendrigan: No, sir.

Bradley: What color were they?

Hendrigan: I have no idea, sir."

Bradley was attempting to show the jury that first, the alleged diaries that Elaine Tyree had kept actually existed. Also, that they were in the apartment when the police arrived. Secondly, he was also instrumental in establishing that police procedure was not followed when they responded to 104 ½ Washington Street on the day of the crime. Had police procedure been correctly followed, Officer Hendrigan could have viewed an inventory sheet of all the items taken out of the apartment and testified as to which officer removed the diaries and where they currently were located. This lapse in judgment and police protocol was only the tip of the proverbial iceberg. Interestingly, Bradley never raised the question as to why a search warrant was not obtained and why documentation of the placement of these items had not been photographed and inventoried, as is done in the natural course of an investigation.

When Earl Michael Peters was called to testify, he had to travel from Fort Bragg as he had been transferred from Fort Devens since testifying at the probable cause hearing. Peters was questioned again about his shotgun. The transcript of that questioning is as follows:

McCormick: Where did you go when you left the barracks that day?

Peters: To his apartment.

McCormick: Do you know the address of his apartment?

Peters: No.

McCormick: It was the apartment you went to earlier?

Peters: Yes, sir, it was on Washington Street, but I don't know the correct address, not just right offhand.

McCormick: When did you go there, sir?

Peters: That evening.

McCormick: That day?

Peters: Yes, it was that evening, between 5:00 and 6:00.

McCormick: When you went there did you get anything?

Peters: Yes, sir.

McCormick: What did you get?

Peters: My shotgun.

McCormick: Would you describe that to us, please?

Peters: It's a Remington 1100, semi-automatic. And it's got a chamber for three-inch Magnums.

McCormick: When did you purchase that, sir?

Peters: It would be the 1st or 2nd of January. It could be the 30th, the 31st. It was one of those four days. I can't recall just right now exactly.

McCormick: Is your memory exhausted relative to what date it was, sir?

Peters: Yes, sir.

Peters seemed to have a difficult time as to the date he allegedly removed the gun from Bill Tyree's apartment. He further testified:

McCormick: After you took your gun from the storage area in the couch, what did you do?

Peters: Took it back to my room, put it in my wall locker. And earlier that morning I got—

McCormick: What morning, sir?

Peters: Monday morning. Yes, sir. I checked it with my platoon sergeant so I could miss formation, so I could check it into the arms room, which is the gun locker on the first floor.

McCormick: -Sir, what did you do with that?

Peters: I signed it into the arms room.

McCormick: That day, sir, Monday following Sunday, what was your duty that day?

Peters: I had security CQ that day.

McCormick: Will you tell us what CQ is, sir?

Peters: That's when you're in charge of quarters and you answer the phones, take any messages. In short, you're in charge of whatever. You're left in charge.

McCormick: What were you in charge of, sir?

Peters: The motor pool that day.

McCormick: What were the hours of your tour of duty that day?

Peters: My hours?

McCormick: Will you tell us the time from when to when, sir?

Peters: From 4:30 early morning, till 8:30, 9:00 Tuesday morning.

McCormick: Will you describe where you were and what you did during that period of time?

Peters: There was snow on the ground and we had to start the trucks every two hours. And as you start the trucks every two hours, then we have three snowplows... I'm sorry, we have four snowplows. We have two 5-ton snowplows, a 2-1/2-ton snowplow, and a 1-1/2-ton snowplow. In between starting all the trucks, I pushed snow in the motor pool and outside the motor pool and along with all that, putting chains on the snowplows, numerous things that pertain to maintenance at motor pool is what your duties would be. As I said, pushing the snow for the next duty day, for the next day when the men come in to work, that everything would be squared away. Also have to clean the office, that type of thing. Make sure the motor pool bays are squared away.

McCormick: And after you finished up with your CQ for that night, where did you go, sir?

Peters: I went to the mess hall.

McCormick: I should say, that morning when you finished up CQ, where did you go?

Peters: I went to the mess hall to eat. Then I went directly to bed.

McCormick: Where was that, sir?

Peters: My room, Service Company, in the second floor, room 255.

Then Bradley went after Earl Michael Peters with a vengeance. He began questioning Peters about statements he had made against Bill Tyree surrounding the Article 15, which he later recanted. Peters denied ever recanting statements while on the stand. He also admitted that he could have had a cot placed in CQ if he had wanted so that he could lie down during the night. This admission was imperative in order to prove that Peters may had been able to rest during the night, rather than not resting as he had claimed until he reached his barracks room the next morning.

Chief Adamson was called to testify about what he witnessed when he first responded to 104 ½ Washington Street in Ayer. He testified, "In the bedroom I observed that there were two dressers, one on each wall. Drawers had been pulled out there." This small statement reflects that the apartment had been ransacked. If someone went to the apartment with the sole purpose of killing Elaine Tyree, why would the dresser drawers be pulled out in the bedroom, especially since she was murdered in the entryway?

Adamson continued to testify about the evening of February 13, 1979, when he arrived at CID. "I was inside the building, downstairs. Many people were around. Within a very few minutes after I arrived, Mr. Tyree came through the door. His face was flushed. He was out of breath. And he said, 'I've just seen the knife, the knife is in the barracks under Aarhus's pillow and you'd better get down there before it's moved,' in words to that effect. He was very excited. At that time, there was further conversation with Mr. Tyree by the other officers." This testimony is in direct contradiction of what William Tyree stated occurred that evening. It is also important to remember that Chief Adamson had been reprimanded during the probable cause hearing for coaching witnesses.

Adamson further testified about the night of February 13, 1979, when Aarhus was brought to the CID office. "On Tuesday, February 13, 1979, between 7:00 and 8:00 p.m., Specialist Erik Y. Aarhus was brought to the second floor, Federal Office, Criminal Investigation Division at Fort Devens, and he was taken to the office of Agent Joseph Burzynski. Present at the time were Agent Burzynski and myself. At that time, we so identified ourselves to Aarhus. I in fact showed my badge and my ID card and he accepted my ID card. I asked Mr. Aarhus if he knew why he had been brought to the CID office and he stated he did not. And at that time, he was advised verbally of his rights under Miranda by myself, in the presence of Mr. Burzynski.

Other law enforcement officers testified about the interrogation of Aarhus as well.

Everyone was in agreement that he appeared to be under the influence of something, since some questions had to be repeated to him. There was also no mention of the drugs that were found in his locker or the alleged blood-stained clothing that had been inventoried by the CID when his room was searched. In fact, these police officials believed they had Elaine's killer under apprehension and none of them thought they should pat him down or search him for a weapon. Again, this was against common police procedure.

On the eleventh day, the Commonwealth had several insurance salesmen testify. They testified that William and Elaine had taken out several policies on Elaine prior to her death. The Commonwealth was attempting to show that Bill was going to profit off of Elaine's death. Mr. Bradley never attempted to explain the reason Bill and Elaine had taken out these insurance policies. Bill claimed the policies were taken out to replace the insurance policy that would end through the United States Army when Elaine was discharged. The insurance agents also testified that Bill never went looking to collect on these policies after Elaine died.

The next witness was CID Agent Joseph Burzynski. He stated, "Sir, to the best of my knowledge, when he (Tyree) first came in, he told me that he had been in contact with Lieutenant Dwyer and Chief Adamson earlier that day. And that he had approached Erik Aarhus about giving him the murder weapon used to kill his wife, Elaine, and that a meeting had been to take place at the Ayer Pizza House Pavilion on Main Street. He said to me that Aarhus was not going to show up at this meeting and that Lieutenant Dwyer and Chief Adamson had been contacted about the meeting not showing up, not taking place. He told me he had gone to the room of Aarhus, talked with him, and had seen what he believed to be the knife used to murder his wife underneath the pillow of Aarhus's bed in the room."

CID Agent Paul Mason was next to testify. He recalled arriving at Service Company barracks on the evening of February 13, 1979. He stated, "Yes, sir, I parked the vehicle in the fire lane. I went into the door, went to the center of the building, which is right near the aisle, and near the commander's office I made a right, went down about ten or fifteen meters, and met with Captain Polcrack, CO. After some discussion, I went down to the end of the hallway. In the vicinity of the arms room, I made a right, went all the way down to the end of the hall, went into the room on the first right at the end of that hallway, assigned living quarters of Erik Aarhus and another individual in the army. I believe his name is Diteman. He was assigned to that room also.

"Well, sir, I was let into the room through a pass key, and opened the door slowly to check to see if there was anybody in the room. Upon entering the room, I made a visual observation of the entire area and then walked over to the bed, which was on the left-hand side. If I could describe it, it would be as you enter the room, the wall locker is there in the room, metal panel wall lockers that are on the left and as you enter the room, took a right, but from the room it would be on the left, which is parallel against the wall. There in the center of the room is, I believe, a stereo and there on that window, and I walked into the room to the bed of Aarhus and picked up the pillow. That's when I saw the plastic bag and the knife."

Mason further testified, "I recognize the knife and sheath to be the articles that I confiscated on the evening of 13 February in the assigned room of Erik Aarhus at approximately 1815 hours." This minor statement that he had taken possession of the knife at 6:15 p.m. is in direct contradiction with the time that Post Commander Colonel Rittgers stated he gave verbal authorization to Agent Burzynski authorizing the search of Aarhus's barracks room. Colonel Rittgers' testimony never wavered that he gave verbal authority for the room search other than at 6:10 p.m. This raises the question as to the validity of the room search and whether or not they had probable cause to search the room.

When Officer Keane testified about a witness who had seen someone running from the apartment at 104 ½ Washington Street around the time of the murder, Bill thought the case was won. Keane stated, "At that time, I believe I was with a couple of other officers and we were just conducting a door-to-door search, if anybody had seen anything in the area. And Mr. Williams lived in an apartment complex next to the scene of the crime. And just in the course of our investigation to talk to everybody that lived in the area, we came upon Mr. Williams. He gave us a description of unknown person."

McCormick asked, "Did the description that Mr. Williams gave you fit the description of Mr. Aarhus?"

Keane replied, "I would have to say no, sir."

Unfortunately, Vias Williams was never called to testify at the probable cause hearing or the trial of Tyree or Aarhus, and the police never followed up on this lead. Years later, Mr. Williams commented on not being called to testify. He reminisced, "I was surprised to find out that there was a subpoena for me in 1980, and that they couldn't find me. Because anybody that's in the military, you can find them worldwide just by making a phone call." Mr. Williams was informed that the authorities had caught the murderer and that they were closing the case and it was over. Had the jury heard his testimony in both trials, it is doubtful either party would have been convicted.

Mr. Bradley began his final arguments by stating, "Madam Forelady, members of the jury, as His Honor has told you, what I say to you now is not evidence, and what Mr. McCormick says to you is not evidence. I guess when we argue to you, we point out things we would like to have you look at in the case, how we would like to have you view the evidence that you have heard, the testimony from that witness stand. Now, as I go through and try to mention the witnesses that you have heard from, and there are many things I would like to suggest to you, I am sure there are one or two things that I'm going to forget. In fact, when I sit down, I'll say, oh, I should have said this or that. It's not my intention on my part to mislead you, it's simply that I have forgotten to say that. At the outset, I would like to say to you that I feel very strongly that nobody should die as Elaine Tyree did. It was a horrid death. A young mother, just brutally killed. But that is done. It is terribly unfortunate. We have to determine now whether or not the Commonwealth, through its witnesses, has introduced enough evidence for you to believe that William Tyree did, in fact, kill his wife.

"Now, we start, I guess, with Mrs. Eliades, the woman who was next door, who heard a blood-curdling scream. She said she called the police. Then she had courage enough to leave her apartment, walk by the apartment where she heard that scream, and wait for the police to come. The police did respond. Mrs. Eliades, prior to telling you that, told you that she looked out a window that had been described, the kitchen window, and she saw Mr. Tyree come up and leave a baby carrier of some description there. She said she didn't see anyone else. He ran in the apartment, ran out, and left.

"Then we had Officer Decott, who responded to a call. Officer Decott said he approached the door. He saw fresh blood on the door and knocked on the door and received no response. He called his chief. His chief came. He made the observations he made, he saw blood on the door and on the floor. At the time Officer Decott went out to call the chief and use the portable Radio, he noticed that the screen that had been in the window when he came up the walk was now laying on the ground near the sidewalk. The window that had been shut was now open. Ultimately, the chief gained admission to the apartment and Officer Decott was dispatched to intercept Mr. Tyree.

"Mr. Tyree, at this time, was at Fort Devens at 441 Military Intelligence Offices or whatever they may have been. He had had some conversation with Captain Klein. If you will remember, Captain Klein said that he thought Tyree was giving him the needle because he had failed to sign in and out when he went to lunch and that he would have some talk with Tyree about time.

"Tyree said to him, 'It's 12:15 p.m., that's about right.' Captain Klein said, 'Yeah, I think so.' He said he looked at the watch, could well have been 12:15 p.m., and that Tyree said it was 12:15 p.m., about 12:15 p.m. right at that moment. Sergeant Henry was in the area, First Sergeant Henry. He testified, I believe he told you, that Tyree got a telephone call and during the telephone call he seemed to him there seemed to be something wrong at Elaine's house. He started to shake all over. Henry said to him, 'Wait a minute, don't leave.' Tyree rushed out the door. I think Sergeant Henry then testified to you that he made a call to the house. I'm not sure of that, it's your memory that counts and not mine. Officer Decott said also that Sergeant Henry told Tyree that he remembered it was 12:15 p.m. Tyree rushed out, got in the truck. After Officer Decott stopped him, Tyree asked him what was going on. What did Decott say? 'This is an investigation. Come with me. We'll take you to the police station.' He told him that and he did take him to the police station. Stayed with him. He said he noticed nothing, no emotion. Didn't answer his questions.

"However, then Lieutenant Boisseau came into the room. I think you remember the landlord situation. He had been to the apartment first and he took, I guess, he took some pictures. Then he went to the police station. He saw Mr. Tyree. He said that he had told him that his wife was dead, had been killed. Originally, he said, 'Ooh, no, no.' But then you recall later on he said, 'Well after I examined him, as a matter of fact, he appeared to be in a state of shock. He had a dazed look and he was making throaty sounds.' Decott said that. Tie this in, if you will, with the testimony here this morning from Captain Carrigan, who was down there about that time. What did the captain say? He didn't know what happened. Tyree didn't know what had happened, was asking—seemed to be upset. 'What is the matter? What is going on?'

"About that time, Trooper Hendrigan joined them. Well, it's interesting here. Lieutenant Boisseau told us that he knew nothing at all about the case. He simply drove him, took him to the police headquarters. And isn't it strange that the sergeant talking to Tyree said to him, 'Your wife is dead. She has been stabbed,' or something like that. Said to him, 'What time did you drive your wife over?' Strange remark from an officer who had no knowledge of what was going on.

"Trooper Hendrigan then joined the scene. Maybe we can come back to that, back to Trooper Hendrigan, and put it together a little bit better. Now, from the same apartment house you heard from the Gibsons. Gibson and the little girl, Julie. They testified to their relationship with the Tyrees,, to both Tyrees. Mrs. Gibson told you that she had had a happy relationship. I think Julie told you pretty much the same thing. She used to go with them sometimes. Billy was driving. Then she babysat. Miss Gibson babysat for them.

Mrs. Gibson said she had feelings of hostility, for the first time, the first time ever. She told you on the witness stand Tyree on the last morning of his wife's death, in the truck going to work, said, 'Yes, we were up with the baby. If that baby were older, I'd beat her.' The first time she ever heard that. Was it fear? Her feelings of hostility? Is that the reason she said it? I don't know. As we leave the Gibsons, what happened at the apartment and immediately at the police station? The officers, all of them, Hendrigan, Dwyer, and Adamson all told you the number of people that they were talking to at the Washington Street address and at the base. They told you all five of them went with Mr. Tyree to the funeral parlor to view his wife's body.

"Trooper Hendrigan said Mr. Tyree moved the sheet down, kissed her on the forehead. Keene said it was the funeral director that removed the sheet. Tyree walked around his wife's body, did kiss the forehead, placed a hand on her forehead. Chief Adamson, of course, saw it differently. Chief Adamson said he saw Tyree pull the sheet down. He walked out of the room saying nothing. He was still in the anteroom. He said Tyree talked fairly normal when he came out and stared at the door, then he put a window in the door after being examined on that and he added the window a little bit later on, because he figured, I supposed, that standing looking at the window, that was not really normal actions.

"Then we had a group of witnesses, starting with Sergeant Neikov. They were present at the funeral of Mrs. Tyree in Cumberland, Maryland about three or four days after the terrible death. I guess the testimony of all, each of them is pretty much along the same lines. Billy Tyree made a fool of himself, he was drunk. In the words of one Sergeant Arena, 'I think he went berserk.' Words of Maguire, 'Appeared to be going crazy.' And somebody else said he did not appear rational at all. I don't recall who that was. There was a conversation, presumably among all of these young people. They were all together. They testified here that at the lounge they were all together. They were all together at the home in Cumberland, talking to Mr. and Mrs. Hebb, the stepfather, stepmother of Elaine. It's interesting to note that one witness said Tyree was going to rent the entire fifth floor of the Holiday Inn and have a big party, only one person of the four that were there heard that and testified to it. I submit for your consideration, if you will, that that does not necessarily mean that the witnesses are lying, but I think we must accept the fact that the murder of Elaine Tyree was a terrible event, an event they all talked about.

"You have been in the position, I suppose, having a big thing happen, whether it be the unfortunate death of somebody by an automobile accident, home accident, or something else, something terrible, something unusual happen. It may be you told your friends when it happened. Four hours later that same story that you told came back to you and you would never recognize it as being the same thing. I think when we get some people, young people at Fort Devens talking as the talk had to be, because witnesses said so, that's what happened. Stories are enlarged and changed, added to. You never recognize them as being the same. But whatever happened in Cumberland, Maryland when he had gone berserk and when he was found in the bathtub of his hotel, what he did say to a girlfriend, he apparently had no clothes on: 'Get out.' We know that he went up to the Walter Reed Hospital in the psychiatric ward. Those records are introduced and you will have them with you and you can read them and see the diagnosis and treatment of Tyree at the Walter Reed Hospital.

"Sergeant Maguire, you were led to believe that Mr. Tyree is supposed to come up and have said, 'I see you're in finance.' He did, in fact, come up and say, 'Are you in finance? There's a problem about insurance. I'm a suspect.'

I would guess that somewhere along the line, somebody was going to pay for this funeral. I see nothing unusual about that question, nothing at all. Mrs. Crabtree testified. Her testimony, I think, went primarily to the music that was selected by William Tyree. 'Dust in the Wind,' 'Tuesday Afternoon,' 'Knights in White Satin,' and 'I'll Go to My Grave Loving You.' I guess that was introduced to show you there was something morbid about somebody selecting music for the funeral. It's done more and more. You know that you can draw from your own experiences from the fact. That music, it's listening music.

"About this time, a fellow named Testagrossa took the stand. Testagrossa, with his willingness to answer questions, his prompt response to anything asked. I think you have the right to consider, you should consider how he answers questions. The only thing he could say is, 'My memory is exhausted,' because as a matter of fact, the first question I asked him on cross-examination. 'My memory is exhausted.' The first, the very first time he came before you and said, 'Oh, yeah, I remember Tyree. He said, "I am going to frame Aarhus, I am going to get a knife, I'm going to put it in the room. I'm going to call the cops." ' Now, is this where it is? It is your memory and not mine that counts. On the first day, when I asked him who first said that to him, my memory is that he told us, 'Oh, I said it to Mr. McCormick the day before.' Then we came back the day after, or Monday after, whatever it may have been, he said, 'Oh, no, the first time I ever said it was right here.' Testagrossa, who told you a great big conversation that some female had with Mr. Tyree in the PX, and he never said it before. Unwilling to answer any kind of questions freely and voluntarily. You can take him for what he is worth.

"The next witness, I think, was cloned from the same group, Peters. Peters unwillingness to answer anything. Reading statements, time after time. Not being willing to answer questions. Peters never telling the police, Burzynski or anyone else, that he heard a conversation from the front door between Mr. Tyree and Aarhus. He did say somewhat later, and I heard bits and pieces, but what he did say to Burzynski, I heard nothing. And he came in here and said, 'Well, I heard more conversation after that. We talked about a Barlow knife.' Never said that to the police or to anyone else. You might question, why would he act that way? Well, let's go back to the apartment for a moment when the police knocked on the door. I submit to you that whoever killed Elaine Tyree, whoever they were, were in that room. The window was open and the screen gone, because somebody went out there is what Adamson says. Couch is open. As to that couch, Peters had stored a Remington shotgun, Remington 1100, 100, whatever it may have been. He told you he took it out on the Saturday or Sunday night before the death. That's what he said. He said that he checked it in to the arms room. He said that he called his sergeant and got special permission to miss the 7:00 a.m. formation to do that, to turn it in.

"We had the armorer come in here, Maxon, who did testify that on another occasion he said that weapon came in at 1430 on January 30. That's about seven and one-half hours after Peters said Tyree was killed, then he changed the time and said, 'Oh, no, no. 0905 on the morning of the 29th.' Daily inventory taken. Sergeant Matthews told you that doesn't show a Remington.

"Then at 0905 on the 29th, it does show a Remington being there at 1430 on the 30th. You heard Peters testify that he bought that shotgun at Herman's. And he had a receipt for the shotgun that he introduced. You will have it. The receipt bears a serial number. Peters said that that is the weapon he had at the apartment. Maxon testified that a monthly inventory was taken on the 30th. There was a Remington there and Lieutenant Hall read off the number of these weapons, including the numbers of the private weapons, privately owned weapons. Those numbers appear on the inventory you will take with you. You can compare those numbers. They are not the same, not even close. Maxon came in here with a green piece of paper, all wrinkled up. 'That is the receipt I gave Peters.' Where did you get the receipt? Out of a trash bag, four months after the weapon was checked, according to him. Four months after, out of a trash bag, a receipt bearing no serial number. He told you he had to put a serial number down, so did Sergeant Matthews. He was then asked, 'Well, how long have you been an armorer?' 'Just a month and a half.' Sergeant Matthews, who handled that arms room, told you that to qualify as being an armorer you went to school, training school, trained is what he said. Maxon, he denied that.

"Peters, I submit for your consideration, has every reason in the world to be an unwilling witness, considering the fact that according to Peters, Tyree at one time said to him, more than one was involved and he wouldn't tell him the name of the second one. Maybe the name was Peters. Peters, pushing a snowplow, a 5-ton snowplow around the parking lot. You will have a photograph in there showing the snow. The police interrogated Mr. Tyree many, many times. You heard them. You heard how many times there were. They never arrested him. Refresh your recollection, how much they forget everything. You heard some talk I consider grossly unfair. Hendrigan and Adamson both testified to you that they had asked Tyree, was she ever separated from you, your wife? Let me ask you, if somebody came up to you and said, 'Ever been separated from your wife or your husband?' I submit that if you had not, did not have a divorce in your background, pending divorce, pending legal separation, you would say no. Would you tell us, 'Well, six months ago, Bill went hunting in Pennsylvania'? No, no, you wouldn't say that. Yes, they would have you believe that, because

Bill denied they were ever separated. When he was in Pennsylvania hunting, his wife was forty-five minutes away visiting her parents in Cumberland, Maryland.

"You heard the testimony of Chief Adamson. You heard how many times Mr. Tyree told Aarhus, 'I'm going to the movies with my wife. We won't be home, we are going out.' And Adamson said, 'Well, he never in so many words said, "I won't be there." ' Does he have to? I suppose if somebody told him something, suggested to you, if you were going to visit them that night, they were going to the movies, they wouldn't be home, you would probably figure out that you shouldn't go there. What about Chief Adamson and the rest of them, when they were quick to ask him about lie detector? At one time he said to them, 'Yeah, I'll answer the question whether I killed my wife.' Later on, what did he say? 'Put me on a polygraph. Put me under hypnosis. Give me truth drugs.' This was never done, never done at all. You will hear later on, I am sure, about why would the police not tell you the truth? They have got nothing to gain. No. I believe, I am sure you will hear that. They have got an interest in the case. You bet your life they have got an interest. They have got an interest in the confession here and don't lose sight of it.

"What about the government theory that Tyree did this for insurance? McCaffrey, the first insurance man, testified that after the baby was born, both Elaine and Bill Tyree approached him and talked about insurance, a family plan. That he put it together. He came up with the amount of money that the budget would stand. He put together the package, he sold it. Bill took it. There was some discussion about did Bill know what he had? Well, Miller testified, the second insurance man. He said that he had to chase Tyree four or five weeks before he could get an appointment. Bill Tyree told him he had insurance. He said, ' am an insurance man. I'll put together something anyway.' He was asked,

'Did Mr. Tyree tell you or did he know what kind of policy he had from McCaffrey?' Mr. Miller said he didn't know. The witnesses that had had any dealings with Mr. and Mrs. Tyree that you have heard from the stand indicated that they were getting along fine; that there were problems prior to the baby being born. He was unhappy with the wife's pregnancy, but that everything had settled down after that, all except for Mary Burton. She was the one he stuck his tongue out at and she figured that was an invite to oral sex. She is the one that said they were not getting along. She and no one else.

"There was introduced yesterday a document supposedly written by Mr. Tyree. The government would have you believe that he wrote it, that everything there is true. What is it? On the day that that document was presented to Officer McHenry, who testified Tyree was out of his cell, he was taken first to the infirmary. He was taken from the infirmary to a local hospital, returned to the infirmary, picked up by a second guard, whose name escapes me and I can't pronounce it anyway, who after a while told you that it was ten, twenty, thirty minutes past ten when he brought Mr. Tyree to the cell. It was 10:30 p.m., ten minutes later, when Mr. McHenry picked up this document and there was no typewriter in the cell. You heard Mr. Richards, the inmate. Incidentally, his record was read in here. But he said to you that night he saw an inmate, I don't remember the name, put a document in Tyree's room. Consider the way Tyree gave this document to McHenry. He called him over, not panicky, not upset. He said, 'Tennessee, come here, I've got something to read to you.' Does that sound like some kind of man reading a dying declaration? The testimony of Mr. Richards, a convict or not, Billerica or not, when he said he saw somebody put it in Tyree's cell, it remains uncontradicted. The Commonwealth wants you to believe that Bill Tyree is cute, smart, cunning— very, very cunning.

That he put this package together, something like Rembrandt where he stood back, made every stroke just so, tinted every color with perfection. He would have you believe that he made Aarhus do this. Said he was going to pay Aarhus to do it. If he is that cunning, or that cute, does it make any sense at all to you that he would then stand around and say that he did it? Don't you think he would be cute enough to realize that anyone in that position would then say, 'He put me up to it'?

"You will hear, I guess, a lot about the terrible things that Mr. Tyree did, the inferences that you will be asked to draw out when you separate the wheat from the chaff. When you look at what these witnesses really and truly have said, consider their manner on the stand. I submit to you that the Commonwealth has failed entirely to prove that the defendant killed his wife. They have to meet the goal of reasonable doubt if they have fulfilled their duty in this case. Again, I would ask you to find him not guilty."

ADA McCormick then stepped out from behind a table, walked over in front of the jury box, and faced them before addressing them. "Madam Forelady, ladies and gentlemen of the jury, it is not my function, as the judge said earlier, to argue on behalf of the Commonwealth. It is sort of a lengthy case. I appreciate very much all the attention that you have given this case A few comments by me, anything that I say here that does not coincide with your recollection of the facts, please disregard what I say.

"The evidence in this case comes from the witness stand and the exhibits that have been presented through the course of this trial. Those are the things that you consider in your deliberations, not what I say or what Mr. Bradley says. It's what you perceive to be the evidence in this case. That is what makes the jury system so wonderful. That is why it lasts in this country, because you good people have had an opportunity now to see both sides. As you have sat there very patiently and observed different witnesses come and go and different exhibits go in and go out, now you people are the judges.

"Now, you people decide upon what you heard and what has been presented in the exhibits It is a situation where you are not asked to close your eyes and put on blinders. When you come into this room, you bring with you all the common sense that you have acquired throughout your lives, all your everyday experiences. You are asked to bring these in here and apply them here. You have judgments to make. You have seen people before and you know how to size a person up. Well, that is precisely what you are going to be asked to do in this case. You are going to be asked to recall the witnesses that testified here. What did they sound like? What did they have to say? How did they respond on cross-examination? How were they on direct examination? What did they say? You are going to be asked to look at all the exhibits and to study the exhibits again, using your good common sense that you have in reaching your verdict.

"Now, as the judge told you, there are two types of evidence: There is direct evidence where a witness takes the stand under oath and says, 'I saw X, Y, Z,' and there is the other type of evidence that you will hear the judge tell you about, and that is circumstantial evidence. The judge will explain what circumstantial evidence is, and he will tell you that it's equal to the direct evidence in this case. He will tell you about vague inferences and how you may not draw the inference, but you may draw reasonable inferences when you are deciding this case. And you may use circumstantial evidence.

"Now, you have an indictment before you. May I see the indictment, Mr. Clerk?" (Clerk hands indictment to counsel.) "You are going to have an indictment before you when you go to the jury room. The indictment is going to read that on such and such a date, William Tyree assaulted and beat one Elaine Tyree with intent to kill her or murder her, and by such assault and beating did kill and murder the said Elaine Tyree. Now, as it was presented in the opening in this case, the Commonwealth is not contending here that William Tyree held that knife in his own hands and put that knife to Elaine Tyree's throat. The Commonwealth is contending two things here: Erik Aarhus was hired to kill Elaine Tyree. The Commonwealth so contends that there was a joint venture, that both these individuals set out and had the intent to kill. Mr. Tyree counseled, procured, or hired Mr. Aarhus to kill Elaine Tyree with malice aforethought and deliberate premeditation. And on that basis, we have spent ten days presenting evidence. Keep those things in mind. Let's just take a brief look at the evidence showing that Erik Aarhus killed Elaine Tyree, that Erik Aarhus killed Elaine Tyree with malice aforethought and deliberate premeditation. Look at the two Green Berets, Mr. Tyree and Mr. Aarhus, both friends, both stationed at Fort Devens, both assigned to the Service Company of the 10th Special Forces. Both, at one time, lived in the same dormitory, both worked together. Keep that fact in mind and direct your attention to January 28, 1979, Sunday afternoon.

"Where is Erik Aarhus? He's in the fire lane at the Service Company barracks, that paved area leading into the back door. Where is Bill Tyree? He's with Erik Aarhus. What are they doing? They are negotiating. About what? Go ahead one day, move forward to January 29, and move forward to that evening.

"Bill Tyree had invited Erik Aarhus over to the house. Never had been there before. Invited him over to the house, but they were going to a movie. Who showed up at the house that night? Erik Aarhus showed up at the house that night. How did he act? Gloves on and off. Nervous. When this young girl came down with the baby, did she leave and go back upstairs again? She went inside that apartment. Why did she go inside that apartment? Was Elaine Tyree afraid? Mr. Aarhus was to do it Monday night. He was to snuff her life out Monday night while Mr. Tyree took himself or joined his friend, Mr. Flores, at a movie. He went down to Service Company barracks and got him an alibi. Erik Aarhus was to do it. But what happened? He didn't. Julie Gibson came downstairs. She threw the wrench in the machine. It didn't happen.

"Move forward one more day, the day that Elaine Tyree was savagely murdered. What happened at the apartment? How did that person get into the apartment? Erik Aarhus, was he brought over there that Tuesday morning at 11:20 a.m. when someone took a baby carrier over there? Who had the key to that apartment? You have heard testimony about keys. Only the Tyrees had keys to that apartment. Well, how did that person get in? You might ask yourselves, was that person in the apartment? Ladies and gentlemen, I direct your attention to Exhibits 15 and 1. I ask you to look closely at that. Do people put rubbish in front of their door or do they put rubbish up in the corner where it belongs? Who moved that rubbish barrel down so they could stand right inside that jog in the wall, so they could stand right there so that when Elaine Tyree walked in that door, they could surprise Elaine Tyree?

"Move on a little bit for now. Move on as the case evolves and you are getting a picture of what happened. Something doesn't fit here. There is no sign of any forced entry. You heard testimony about the area here, the window. There are no signs of a forced entry. What happened? Someone is questioned because there are lot of questions. What happened? Lo and behold, on February 13, 1979, two weeks to the day, this knife appears. This knife with 'Captain Beyond' on it, Aarhus's nickname. It appears in Aarhus's room and under Aarhus's pillow. Lo and behold, what kind of blood is on this knife? Type B- blood. How does this knife fit in with the wounds? What did the chemist say as the length of that knife? Did Erik Aarhus kill Elaine Tyree? Is there any question? Now, the question: Did Bill Tyree hire or procure or counsel Erik Aarhus to kill Elaine Tyree? Or did he jointly participate in the murder? Back up. Now go back in time a little bit. Look at his actions that Sunday, when he was with Erik Aarhus and they were negotiating. Now, go to the Monday when he told Julie Gibson he had an appointment with his first sergeant that night. Where did he go? He didn't go to the first sergeant; he went to the movies. He went to the movies with Flores so that if they ever asked him the question, 'Did you kill your Wife?' he could say, 'I didn't kill my wife.'

"Go on a little bit further to the day of the killing. These police officers, they have got a job to do. They know how to do it. They see a situation; they see a crime scene, and questions arise. The first question they started asking Mr. Tyree on the 30th of January: Account, sir, for your time. Where were you? Went to work. Had to go take some typewriters. Talked about some sort of military court. Brought my wife home. I had to get back to bring the typewriters back because my first sergeant would have my whatever he said it was. That is what he said. He said, on top of that, you talk to Lieutenant Klein. He knows that I was there. The man got his alibi.

"But now, go into it a little bit further. You've heard the witnesses; you have heard what they testified to. Bring the typewriters back. You heard the testimony. Henry tripped over them that morning. He came in there at 10:30 a.m. and he made a note. He wrote it out on a piece of paper. Tyree, the typewriters, what are they doing here? Beecham helped him unload the typewriters at lunchtime. Beecham came out of the shed, came across, they talked about the truck, the four-wheel truck. He will tell you he carried them in between 10:30 a.m. and 11:00 a.m. What was his big hurry after he dropped his wife off and tooted the horn a couple times? Then he said, 'Never mind, I've got to get going,' whatever... What was the toot of the horn, ladies and gentlemen?

"Then what happened back at the 441st Military Intelligence Detachment building? He was never there at lunchtime, that's what Sergeant Henry said. But he was there this day. And he is just not there. He comes back in the back door. 'Lieutenant, does 12:15 sound right?' Lieutenant going to remember that, isn't he? No matter what he said it for. He said it to get the time across to that lieutenant, because he knew what was happening at his house when he tooted that horn and he knew that it would be important for him to have an alibi. Remember what the lieutenant said? The lieutenant's desk was way over in the corner, out of the way. He got the furthest spot in the building so that he wouldn't be bothered by anybody. He was sort of ducking things. No offense to the lieutenant. Who appears at his desk? Just happened to have walked over to have a conversation? Bill Tyree. Why?

"Henry remembered what Bill said, 'Oh, gotta call my wife.' It's ten minutes of one, whatever it was. Doesn't call from there, he goes downstairs. Top Sergeant Henry, 'Hi, Tyree.' The typewriters, he doesn't pay any attention to Top Sergeant Henry. His superior officer is talking to him. He doesn't pay any attention; he keeps right on going into a room in the back. Did he keep on going, ladies and gentlemen, because he knew what was going to happen when he called the house, and he was going to be able to say to Sergeant Henry that there was no answer, or there's trouble at my house? He didn't even know what the trouble was.

"Chief Adamson talked to him on the phone, said that there had been a problem. 'You'd better come out. I want you to leave.' Then he started shaking, not even knowing whether it might be a broken window. He knew what it was all about. He knew right at that moment when he had the phone in his hand that Erik Aarhus had completed his task that he set out to do, and that was to kill Elaine Tyree.

"Move on. The police talked to Bill Tyree. What about being up to the apartment that morning, earlier, with the baby carrier? Oh, forget that, yes, because someone in the apartment building had seen him there, a lieutenant.

"Then you have heard all the evidence relative to the different statements, relative to when he made the first statement, as to when he made the second statement, Vietnam veteran of some eight or eleven months. But you come to find out that is not true. What does that show you? What does that indicate? What kind of smokescreens are being set up in here? Now, you have the conversation on the 31st in which he sits down again. I am not going to touch everyone, we have had ten days' worth of evidence, so I don't intend to touch upon everything But then you have the interview on the 31st in which, by the way, was Aarhus out to the house? Oh, yes, he was there Monday night. Why? Well, we were going to talk over something, but then I told him that I was going to the movies. Well, did you tell him that you were and not to come out? I told him I was going to the movies.

"I think it was February 9, he was asked at the colonel's office and he goes over to the Ayer Police station and he has a chat with Chief Adamson. 'I will take a polygraph.' Sure, you will take the polygraph. 'I will answer one question.' What? 'I will answer one question. Did I kill my wife?' Grieving husband. A grieving husband? What did he do, ladies and gentlemen, when he made that statement? 'I will answer one question.'

"Then move on to February 12. You heard the chief of police reading that statement. You have had an opportunity to size up basically what the conversation was about. I think it was suggested by counsel for Mr. Tyree that they were putting pressure on, they were putting heat on Mr. Tyree. I must agree, they were. They have had three interviews. Statements have changed. How did that person get in the house? How did that person visit Elaine? And they started to focus in. And I think—strike that, not what I think—and from that interview you can tell that the pressure began to go on Bill Tyree. What happened? What happened after the police finished questioning on that day? He knows who murdered his wife. He participated with that murderer. What happened? What happens? The perfect crime, ladies and gentlemen? I will tell the police who did it. I will give them Aarhus, and I will get Aarhus to bring the knife back.

"Doesn't it seem strange, two weeks later, that Aarhus still has the murder weapon with the blood on it? What is he holding it for? Is he waiting for payment from Bill Tyree? How did Bill Tyree get him to bring the knife to the pillow? I will take the spotlight off myself and I will give them Mr. Aarhus. That is precisely what he did. And you heard it, ladies and gentlemen, and I submit to you this is exactly what he was relying on. Wouldn't I be crazy if I was involved in it, to put the spotlight on Aarhus? Not really, because who would suspect me of putting the spotlight on somebody if I had something to do with it? Another smoke screen. Another story, another version. Ask any of those military witnesses that you heard testify, he is a soldier. He is a good soldier. He's good for details. He is outstanding. He had a mission to accomplish. His mission was to terminate his wife's life. What happened? When he said the knife was under the pillow, what happened? If he didn't do this with Erik Aarhus, how would he ever get Erik Aarhus to put that knife under the pillow?

"You will also have a statement that Bill Tyree made on the evening of Tuesday, February 13, the evening that they found the knife in Mr. Aarhus's room. I ask you to look at that statement. I ask you to look at the handwriting on that statement. What does it say in that statement? $5,000 of the insurance money I promised him. Was the $5,000 to kill his wife or was the $5,000 to bring the knife back? Well, on January 26, 27, I'm reading from Exhibit 25 Sunday, January 27, 1979, he was at the Service Company barracks when he stated that unless I give him $3,000, he would go instead to the CID. Well, $25 is one thing, but $3,000 .Damn, my wife would miss that much for certain. He is telling you a new story. He is now telling them that Aarhus ,on the night of the 13th, was extorting money from him. I point that out to you, ladies and gentlemen, but more importantly I point out to you what it says here. Sunday, January 27, from his own statement he was with Aarhus at the barracks. Is there any question they were the in fire lane? Says so in the letter. I ask you to peruse this. See what kind of mind writes that kind of letter. Now, look back for just a couple minutes. Now, we've got to the point where the knife has been recovered. The blood is still on it. Now, look back and ask yourself what is indicated? What could the Commonwealth show that indicates that he did do something like this?

"Go back to November of 1979, in the parking lot of his apartment building and talking with Earl Peters. He is his friend. Spent a lot of time with him. Keep that in mind. These people that came in and testified here, were they friends of his? Did they find it difficult to come forward? Can you hit a moving target at fifty-five miles an hour on Route 495? What? Can I roll my truck over the hill? Where do I get to some mountains to roll my truck over the hill so I can get out of it and my wife won't? What about a hired assassin? So, the beginning of January, can I get one in Boston? What about Beecham, his acquaintance over at the military detachment? They talked about four-wheel drives. What did he say to Beecham? Beecham thought he was joking, but what did he say to Beecham? 'I was up on a hill, I could have almost tipped the truck over, and my wife would have gotten killed.' What about Bill Tyree? What about looking back? What was the situation? The marriage was unstable. What about the marriage? Excuse me, just for a moment. Take a look at Exhibits 37 and 38, two letters. Exhibit 37, written to Mr. Tyree, Exhibit 38, a letter found in Mr. Tyree's apartment, up on top of the refrigerator in a coffee can, signed by Bill Tyree. Again, take a look at the document he signed the night they retrieved the knife from Aarhus's room and take a look at this and take a look at what this says. Take a look at what he is saying. 'If she wasn't pregnant, I would be single again.' Take a look where it says, 'Nope, I ain't had VD yet, but I don't know why not.' Just take a look at what it says about going to Alaska for eighteen months and cooling down. 'I figured that out to break up my marriage and nothing else.' Does this sound like a man who was concerned about his wife?

"I direct your attention to these letters. I suggest, ladies and gentlemen, that taking all this evidence, not just the incident down in Maryland, albeit everybody reacts differently to some sort of grief, but 'Tuesday Afternoon' by the Moody Blues, he doesn't know what he was doing? He went crazy down in Maryland? Take a look at that closely. He wasn't acting properly, that is for sure. You heard the testimony. You heard Sergeant Henry say everybody was hot and down on who? Mr. Tyree. Yes, they knew he wasn't acting properly down in Maryland. How do you straighten it out? Try to get attention, try to get attention?

"Get Arena up. Arena said get to bed, get out of the tub. Notice that situation, if he's going crazy, if he is so drunk, why is he concerned about the young lady standing there at the bathtub when he has no clothes on from the waist down? Does that sound like someone that's crazy? He is saying, 'You, get out of here. I don't want you here because I'm not fully clothed.' Then what happened? When Sergeant Henry left the room, Sergeant Henry told them to lock the door. He locked the door. He is in the room by himself. Still no attention. And now he understands that he's not talking properly. What should I do? Well, take the chair and break it, because that's what happened, the chair was broken. Then called the desk, which he remembers calling, and have them come up and say someone attacked me. But what happens now? How did the police officer get in the room? The police officer is there to kick the door down because he had the night latch on it. Again, somebody who doesn't know what he's doing? How did he react to the police officer down there in Maryland when the police officer tried to help him out? What does that sound like? I'll break your collarbone, left first, right second. And he says to the nurse, I'll do the same to you. Why? Why was he so concerned unless he and Aarhus have just killed his wife and remember, if you have a hospital record from the Walter Reed, and you will read the records, you will have an opportunity to see what he said, what they said, and how they treated him based upon what he said, but go back to the night that the murder happened.

"That Monday night—strike that—Tuesday night on the 30th, when Sergeant Henry went down and picked him up and brought him up and put him in the commander's office, put him on the couch in there and let him down and he went to sleep. He slept like a lamb. What did he say to the company commander the next morning? I didn't sleep. But Sergeant Henry saw him. Sergeant Henry checked him. What does he say about what he is saying? Just in summing up, ladies and gentlemen, you have a situation where you have all these factors to consider. What reason did Aarhus have to kill her? Who had a reason? Who was hostile with Elaine Tyree? Who was having marital problems with Elaine Tyree? Who, according to Captain Carrigan, was having financial problems? Who just suffered a financial loss? The letter dated June 16, 1979. What did he do on January 17, 1979, a fellow who suffered a financial loss? Takes on an additional insurance policy. He's got a $20,000 policy on Elaine, got a $20,000 policy from the Service, $22,000 policy with Allstate, and they go on buying more insurance policies, which is going to pay $40,000 on a woman who's not going to be working any longer.

"Take a look at Exhibit 41, Elaine Tyree's orders. On January 29, 1979, Elaine Tyree got her orders. She was discharged as of February 2, 1979. She was going to be a financial drain on William Tyree. William Tyree had the means to terminate her life. When he drove her out there on Tuesday at 12:00 p.m.—and he was very careful it was 12:00 p.m.—Officer Decott said 12:04 p.m. when the call came in, and at 12:00 he was leading a lamb to slaughter. It was as if, ladies and gentlemen, that he planted a bomb in that apartment and he was letting his wife go in there and that bomb exploded. Thank you very much."

With final arguments made, the judge instructed the jury and dismissed them so that they might start deliberating Bill's fate.

***

On the fifteenth day after the trial began, the jury reached a verdict after deliberating for a day and a half. The transcript of the trial is as follows:

The clerk: As to Indictment 79-1398, charging William Tyree, Junior with murder, what say you, Madam Forelady, is the defendant guilty or not guilty?

The Forelady: The defendant is guilty as charged.

The clerk: Guilty of what?

The Forelady: As charged.

The clerk: Members of the jury, you will harken to the verdict as recorded by the Court. The jury upon oath says the defendant is guilty of first-degree murder, so say you, Madam Forelady?

The Forelady: Yes.

The clerk: So say you all, members of the jury?

The jury: Yes.

The Court: Ladies and gentlemen, you may be seated. At this time, I most sincerely thank you for your service on this jury. I am going to excuse you now and I will come back in the jury room to express my thanks to you for your service personally. I do say to you on the record that now the case is over, while you have every right to comment on anything that you saw and heard during the course of the trial, I strongly suggest—I do not order you, but strongly suggest—that you do not, because what went on in this jury room with anyone, that is private to you, the jurors in this case, and you should not discuss that with anyone. It helps preserve the integrity of the jury system. The jury is now excused and I will remain on the bench.

Bill was taken from the courthouse to Massachusetts Correctional Institute Cedar Junction, Walpole, Massachusetts, to serve a life sentence for murder. Bill recalls his thoughts after being convicted: "First the action of defending Earl Michael Peters against the criminal complaints issued by Judge Killam in 1979 constituted a conflict of interest, as this action of defending Peters went as far as to file pleadings on behalf of Peters, which violated Massachusetts General Laws Chapter 268A, as cited in the facts. The question raised is whether or not GLC 268A was violated through the act of the district attorney filing official pleadings on behalf of Earl Michael Peters, who was not a state employee but a person declared a criminal defendant by Judge Killam in the same criminal case. The fact that the office of the Middlesex District Attorney will defend Peters to whatever lengths are necessary to prevent the arrest of Peters. This fact lends credibility to the letter between Droney and Cutolo.

"Secondly, allowing the surveillance of the First District Court of Northern Middlesex County to continue after there was reasonable knowledge to believe the surveillance existed as early as April 10 or 11, 1979, which was sufficient grounds to obtain a search warrant, constituted a conflict of interest. The conflict of interest on this is twofold. First, the conflict of interest is seen as the office of the district attorney disregarded the law (state and federal wiretap statutes), when the district attorney failed to stop the surveillance as soon as it was known to exist; and to preserve the evidence of the surveillance, i.e., the cassette tapes destroyed by A.D.A. Hardoon. Secondly, the motivation of Droney to disregard the ongoing surveillance which was known to exist, and which was sufficiently present as to support the request for a search warrant for the court, was a conflict of interest. The motivation of D.A. Droney could substantiate the letter between Cutolo and Droney."

"I was certainly naïve about the judicial system in America. There's a lot of people who are in prison who are innocent. The system is very flawed." Sam Rockwell

INTERLUDE

Although the factual matrices of murder cases vary greatly, certain themes run through them. When a wife is killed by what appears to be criminal means, the husband (unless he has an ironclad alibi) is the first to be scrutinized if no other suspect appears on the horizon. The police will pursue the husband recklessly to solve the crime. This is because nearly one-third of murdered women die at the hands of their husbands, ex-husbands, or boyfriends, according to FBI statistics. More than half of these women are married, and guns are the weapon of choice. The FBI Behavioral Science Unit would contend that tempers and finances fuel these figures. Investigators would contend that the husband is always the suspect because of statistical probabilities. A good percentage of women are killed by someone they know and in addition, something specific about the case may suggest who the murderer is. So, it shouldn't have come as a surprise to anyone why Bill Tyree was under suspicion and being pursued by law enforcement.

Most interpersonal crimes are motivated by a combination of reasons. Some are financially motivated, maybe jealousy or the husband is abusive... The list can go on and on. Some are motivated by passion, where explosive anger and rage play a part. Others more methodical, calculating, and planning.

When it comes to the trial process in the United States, most Americans receive their knowledge from television shows such as *Perry Mason, Law & Order*, or some derivative of them. The American public hears about some horrific murder and when the police make an arrest in the case, the public feels that justice has been done and they can again feel safe. To the public, an arrest implies solution, the general feeling that law enforcement has done its job. They do not equate jury acquittal with innocence. The defendant, if innocent, believes that he will be exonerated by our judicial system and his life will return to normal. This is almost never the case. Even if he is exonerated of the charges, the public has already found him guilty, because most Americans believe that the police do not arrest innocent people. The American justice system does not neatly wrap up a case in an hour as it does on television. Guilt, like most things, is scarcely ever black and white. As the wheels of justice grind on, innocence becomes progressively less relevant and most innocent defendants realize this.

Bill Tyree was a young man who had little to no discernment when it came to choosing his friends. Once he became aware of what was taking place at Fort Devens and what the guys he hung around with were doing, he should have immediately distanced himself and his family from them. However, a lack of discernment does not make one guilty of murder. Secondly, once this heinous crime was committed, he should have retained competent legal counsel. This act of omission was more than likely due to his age and naivety in the belief that only guilty people need lawyers.

The first thing a defense attorney attempts to establish is a timeline to the crime. The timeline is a compound alibi, where no one witness can prove that the defendant was not at the scene of the crime, but a combination of witnesses and circumstances can preclude the possibility that the defendant had an opportunity to commit the crime. In this case, the killer had to take some time to stash the bloody clothes so well that to this day they have never been found, then go and shower. The timeline is usually the largest puzzle piece in a criminal case.

Secondly, let's look at Bill Tyree's demeanor. Not even Sir Laurence Olivier himself could have killed a person in cold blood then, minutes later, appear in various groups acting casual and relaxed. Tyree was anything but nervous or tense. All this changed once he learned what had happened. It was at this time he became distraught, fidgeting, eyes darting to and fro. Was this an extraordinary piece of acting deserving of an Oscar? Or was it, in truth, the natural conduct of one who was in the catbird seat and suddenly descended into hell? Thirdly, Tyree was questioned almost immediately. He was grilled by the seniormost officers and detectives of the Massachusetts State Police and the Ayer Police Department.

It is doubtful that a guilty layman—or even an experienced criminal—could have made it through those interrogations without slipping up one or more times.

Bill Tyree's and Eric Aarhus's defense counsels both lacked the solid pre-trial investigations that are the cornerstone of a solid criminal defense. Defense counsels may have thought they turned over every rock but obviously, they had not. If they had done their due diligence in their investigative work, they would have been able to show that the culture at Fort Devens during this time was fraught with tension and criminal activity. A simple talk with the US Army Intelligence and Security Command would have revealed that during the late 1970s and early 1980s, there were multiple reports and ongoing investigations at Fort Devens. These investigations centered around subversion and sabotage against the US Army (SAEDA), Security Management Information (SMI). By bringing this to light at trial, defense counsel would have been able to raise doubt in the minds of the jury as to the competency of the CID and its agents and military personnel who testified. Investigators should have checked the serial numbers of all military and personal weapons in the 10th Special Forces Group (A) arms room. This would have been beneficial to possibly discrediting Peters when he testified about the serial number of his shotgun. Tyree's defense counsel never considered the possibility that the serial number he gave may have been attached to a military weapon rather than the Remington shotgun.

Another major aspect in this case was that these two defendants were tried and convicted first in the court of public opinion. Both men were duly charged and put on trial in what could only be viewed as a venomous atmosphere. It can be argued that the newspapers and news media publicity before and during the trial could have been sufficient to compel the conclusion that both defendants' civil rights were violated. Freedom of the press is a cherished freedom, but it cannot be permitted to overshadow the rights of an individual to a fair trial. The courts should have had a change of venue in an attempt to maintain jurors' impartiality because of the publicity and since the court didn't suggest it, the defense attorneys should have argued for it. Besides the media circus surrounding this case, the defense attorneys should have also realized that many of the people living in the area were retired and former military who viewed many of the army personnel assigned to Fort Devens as sub-par soldiers due to the quality of the draftees during the Vietnam War. This unrealistic view by the local citizens also played a major role in muddying the waters of the potential jury pool. A defense attorney not only has to win in the courtroom but also in the court of public opinion. They need to demonstrate that their clients are being unjustly accused in order to sway public opinion in their favor.

Another disturbing aspect to this case was the courtroom skills of the defense attorneys.

Unfortunately, the art of cross-examination is not taught in law schools across America to the extent that it is needed. Defense attorneys, through cross-examination, must be able to destroy the evidence amassed against the defendant. They must diminish it, limit it, and explain it away. Most defense attorneys do not realize that the cross-examination of expert witnesses such as police officers and CID agents poses added problems. An expert witness is a professional who understands the trial process better than most trial attorneys. They know how much they can get away with and how to answer questions, and they are also well versed in this field. When police officers give false testimony, their dishonesty usually stems from an attempt to cover up shoddy police work Other reasons range from a lack of willingness to do their jobs thoroughly and appropriately to a simple desire to convict suspects whom they believe are guilty. In Tyree's case, CID agent Burzynski had a personal vendetta against him due to their prior meetings. The Ayer Police Department was definitely attempting to cover up shoddy police work. A skilled defense attorney would have been able to expose Agent Burzynski's personal biases against Tyree, which would have brought doubt on his testimony and truthfulness as an impartial investigator.

Police coercion usually creeps in during the part of the investigation process when police have the task of interrogating suspects and eliciting confessions. Sometimes, officers inadvertently or purposefully influence the statements of both witnesses and suspects. The issue of coercion surrounding the CID statements of both Tyree and Aarhus, as well as the mental state of Erik Aarhus when he was taken into custody most certainly should have been addressed in both trials. It is with absolute certainty that the last word in this book will not be the last word in this case.

I know there are many well intentioned people out there who are reading this book and saying to themselves that with all of these blatant errors, Tyree and Aarhus can appeal their convictions and get their sentences overturned. It seems simple enough. We have all seen movies and TV shows where this happens and justice prevails. Unfortunately, the judicial system is not that simple. There is no doubt that this method is an innocent man's best chance post-conviction, yet this is a notoriously difficult task.

In the austere world of appeals, oral arguments are fluff. They serve as entertainment for justices who spend most of their time toiling over legal minutia. Legal briefs are the precision weaponry in modern appellate warfare. Appellate judges are unsympathetic to appeals on fairness. Most times, on appeal, facts are overwhelmingly construed in the favor of the government. Appellate justices are only concerned with one thing: viable legal issues.

Legal issues are essentially the trial judge's mistakes: misstatements of law, violations of process, failure to conform to the dictates of appellate court opinions, and breaches of constitutional dimension. In order to be successful on appeal, the criminal defense attorney must correctly identify these issues, cite a dozen or so appellate court decisions that support his contention, and persuasively argue that this issue alone or in combination with other issues has denied his client an impartial procedurally correct trial as guaranteed by the Sixth Amendment of the US Constitution or the Massachusetts Declaration of Rights.

In order for an attorney to spot these issues, he must be extremely well versed in criminal law, procedure, and appellate court precedent going back over at the last two hundred years. In other words, when a trial judge needs to apply an appellate court interpretation to a unique factual circumstance that is before them, they often are confronted with conflicting appellate court opinions that can result in an honest trial judge running afoul by applying the wrong appellate court opinion by applying the dictates of another.

When this occurs, it falls on a seasoned appellate attorney to identify these trial court errors—and herein lies the difference between an appellate attorney and an ordinary criminal defense attorney.

"The fundamental problem is that there's no credibility in the judicial system, which is a system that's been completely politicized. This is retaliation and selective repression." Leopoldo Lopez

CHAPTER EIGHT

The Cruelties of Fate

Bill immediately appealed his conviction. Unfortunately, it was to no avail. The Commonwealth reviewed the case from April 5, 1982, till August 23, 1982. The Honorable Judge Lynch released his twenty-two-page decision and addressed every point that Bill and his lawyers raised questions on. Ultimately, his appeal was denied.

On Aarhus's appeal, Judge Young stated, "Upon this evidence, I find independently of the motion judge that the Commonwealth had met its heavy burden of establishing the voluntariness of the confession and the knowing, intelligent, and voluntary waiver by Aarhus of his Miranda rights. With the exception of the sentence quoted in the text from Paragraph Four of the motion judge's findings and the last sentence of that same paragraph, I adopt his findings and rulings verbatim. Motion for reconsideration is, therefore, denied."

After Bill's conviction and denial of his appeal, he received a letter from Elaine's father. Enclosed with the letter was a copy of a letter Mr. Hebb had received from Assistant District Attorney Lawrence McCormick on letterhead from District Attorney John Droney's office. That letter, dated March 13, 1980, is as follows:

Dear Mr. Hebb,

Your Correspondence of March 4, 1980, to the office of the Middlesex District Attorney has been referred to me for response.

You have previously informed me of the contents of the correspondence in question. I would remind you of two things. The conviction of William Tyree Jr. on February 29, 1980, is currently under appeal, and you are counting on the money from the insurance policies to pay for the additions to your home. You need those additions to provide a place for your granddaughter to live. If you go to Judge Young with your information you will not only jeopardize the conviction, but will prolong or ultimately forfeit any chance you will have in obtaining custody of your granddaughter and the insurance money. If you still desire to speak to Judge Young after you review this letter, I will consider your request. At this point and time, I discourage you from that course of action.

If there is any question or problem, please call. You have my number.

The letter was signed by Assistant District Attorney Lawrence McCormick.

In 1982, Bill Tyree began examining every aspect of his case. He began studying the law in the law library in prison. He noticed that the Ayer Police Department and Massachusetts State Police did not obtain a warrant to search his apartment or remove Elaine's body from the apartment. This was a major point that should have been raised by his ineffective counsel at the probable cause hearing as well as at trial. This struck him as odd, since the courthouse was only down the street from where he resided, and obtaining warrants were standard police procedure. He decided to file a lawsuit against Chief William Adamson, the Town of Ayer, Patrick Keane, and Roderick Hendrigan.

The complaint is as follows:

"The plaintiff, William Tyree Jr., is a resident of MCI Walpole, Massachusetts Correctional Institution. The defendant, William Adamson Sr., was the police chief of Ayer, Massachusetts, until 1981. William Adamson Sr. resides at Douglas Drive, Ayer, Massachusetts, County of Middlesex. Ayer, Massachusetts is a town in the Commonwealth of Massachusetts with the responsibilities and duties in securing a police organization. Patrick Keane, the defendant, is a State police officer assigned to the Middlesex District Attorney Office at the Middlesex Courthouse, East Cambridge, Massachusetts. William Adamson Sr., the Ayer Police Chief on January 30, 1979, was responsible for the Tyree homicide investigation. The homicide took place in Ayer, Massachusetts. William Adamson Sr. testified numerous times under oath that during the course of his investigation he entered the Tyree apartment at 104 1/2 Washington Street, Ayer, Massachusetts, Apartment 1, from January 30, 1979, until the middle of February 1979. Defendant Adamson Sr. also testified that he possessed a set of keys to the apartment which he had made up. Patrick Keane concluded on his testimony on direct examination by stating that he had on numerous occasions after the death of Elaine Tyree gone into the Tyree apartment (Trial Transcript 1664).

"Around January 31 or February 1, 1979, Keane found numerous papers, letters, et cetera (Trial Transcript 1665). I found them in a coffee can in the cabinet about the refrigerator (Trial Transcript 1665). Two of the letters which he took from the coffee can were offered into evidence by the prosecutor (Trial Transcript 1665-1666). Two of the letters were admitted as Exhibits 37 and 38. Exhibit 1: Roderick Hendrigan admitted under oath that he removed diaries and other materials from the Tyree apartment during the course of his investigation. Exhibit 2: The police did not secure a search warrant during the entire course of their investigation of the Tyree homicide. Exhibit 3: The police have never submitted an inventory of what items were taken out of the Tyree apartment during the course of their investigations.

"Police Chief William Adamson Sr. resigned from office on November 3, 1981, due to citizen concern about severe internal problems within the department and that it was 'in the best interest of the town.' On the weekend of February 25, 1980, vandalism exceeding $20,000 was done at the Ties SanVel Construction Company, Westford Road, Littleton, Massachusetts This episode took place during the week of the Tyree murder trial. The Attorney General of the Commonwealth of Massachusetts has initiated an investigation into the allegations of the references that Adamson Sr. hid copies of the reports on the Ties vandalism in his desk for two years without notifying proper authorities of the documents. William Adamson Sr. attempted to dismiss Ayer policeman Stanley Randall because of his role in the State Attorney General's investigation of four police officers. The Town of Ayer's citizens overwhelmingly blocked Adamson's attempts to terminate Randall, and all charges were dismissed. The four Ayer policemen questioned about the vandalism sought the services of former District Attorney McCormack, the prosecutor in the Tyree trial.

COUNT ONE TORT OF TRESPASS TO PROPERTY: The plaintiff incorporates by reference Paragraphs One through Twenty-three. The defendant has conducted a two-week warrantless search of the Tyree apartment. The fact that a homicide occurred did not, of itself, give rise to such exigent circumstances as to justify a warrantless search. The factor that Tyree was arrested did not in any manner lessen his privacy right to his apartment. Tyree, by being a murder suspect, did not forfeit his expectations to privacy or constitutional protected rights of privacy. The Fourth Amendment reflects those who wrote the Bill of Rights that the privacy of a person's home and property may not be totally sacrificed in the name of maximum simplicity in enforcement of the criminal law.

COUNT TWO CONVERSION: The plaintiff incorporates by reference Paragraphs One through Twenty-three. The police and defendants conducted a two-week warrantless search of the Tyree apartment, removing many items. None of the items in the apartment that were removed were inventoried. William Tyree Jr. was never notified what was removed or what was examined in the apartment. The protection of the Fourth Amendment consists in requiring that the usual inferences from evidence be drawn by a neutral and detached magistrate instead of being judged by the officer engaged in the often competitive enterprise of ferreting out crime. The items taken out of the Tyree apartment during the warrantless search were not inventoried or returned to Tyree. The courts have a duty to examine and make an independent evaluation of what is removed for the record.

COUNT THREE TORT OF INVASION OF PRIVACY: The plaintiff incorporates by reference Paragraphs One through Twenty-three. The factor that Tyree, as a murder suspect, does not forfeit his expectations to privacy of home or other constitutionally protected areas the extensive nature of the warrantless search without any inventory filed could not be justified in any manner.

COUNT FOUR BAD FAITH INTERFERENCE WITH TYREE'S CONSTITUTIONAL RIGHTS AND HIS RIGHTS UNDER MASSACHUSETTS DECLARATION OF RIGHTS: The plaintiff incorporates by reference Paragraphs One through Twenty-three. There is a concealment of documents removed from the Tyree home by experienced police officers in a major homicide. The warrantless search resulted in a bad faith interference with Tyree's constitutional rights.

COUNT FIVE TORT OF MISFEASANCE, NON-FEASANCE AND MALFEASANCE OF POLICE DUTIES: The defendants, in removing articles from Tyree's home without a search warrant in a homicide matter, can be characterized as a professional lack of judgment, absence of common sense, disingenuousness, partial truths and candor with the court. These experienced law enforcement officials, who had every opportunity to reach an impartial magistrate there is always the assumption that there may have been motive not to provide an inventory to an impartial magistrate. THEREFORE, the plaintiff demands judgment against the defendants in the sum of $500,000.00 in damages, plus interest, costs and reasonable attorneys' fees.

Chief Adamson was questioned about one incident that he and Officer Keane had searched the apartment at 104 ½ Washington Street:

Question: And about what time did you observe Officer Keane in the apartment on the 30th?

Adamson: I don't know, probably between 12: 00 p.m. and 2:00 p.m.

Question: Did you notice Keane looking for documents in the apartment or searching the apartment?

Adamson: I don't know what he was doing.

Question: Did you see him near the refrigerator in the Tyree apartment?

Adamson: Yes, I did.

Question: And what did you observe Officer Keane doing near the refrigerator in the Tyree apartment? Looking in the general area, what was on top of the refrigerator, what was on top of counters?

Adamson: He took something or found something.

Question: What did he find in a coffee can?

Adamson: He said they were letters.

Question: Do you know what Officer Keane did with those letters?

Adamson: No, sir.

Question: Did you see him leave the apartment with those letters?

Adamson: I saw him leave the apartment. I don't know whether he had the letters or not.

It is widely believed that Massachusetts State Police officer Keane found the diaries that Elaine kept and removed them from the apartment. The illegal search of 104 ½ Washington Street began on the day of the murder, January 30, 1979 and continued until February 21, 1979, until the police gave back the key to the apartment. During this time frame, the police were showing up whenever they wanted and taking anything they felt like without ever having to log it into evidence or onto an inventory sheet. When the judge rendered his verdict in this case, he stated to Chief Adamson that he could have overlooked him not getting a search warrant for the first couple days due to the nature of the case. However, to never obtain a search warrant was a clear violation of Mr. Tyree's civil rights. This was the first time that the police were proven to have dropped the ball with this case.

In 1987, Gaye Tyree, Bill's mother, decided that she would swear out a complaint against Earl Michael Peters for the murder of her daughter-in-law, Elaine. Bill recalls, "Following a closed-door hearing by Special Appointed Magistrate Cotter, all charges against Earl Michael Peters were either dropped or dismissed in general. And my own other accused the Middlesex district attorney of actually defending Peters, who isn't a State employee. Further, when my mother took an appeal before Orange District Court Justice Jablohnski, again the hearing was closed to the public, and again, Peters was defended by the district attorney, and again Mr. Peters walked away scot-free, unable to be prosecuted."

One of the biggest discoveries Bill's mother made was while attempting to have Peters arrested, and it came from her own investigation. She spoke with Bill's former landlord, Mr. Gardner, who had opened the door for the police at 104 ½ Washington Street.

Mr. Gardner stated, "Shortly after noon on the 30th of January, 1979, I was called to one of my rental units by the police. They had received a report of trouble at 104 ½ Washington Street. As we approached the driveway at that address, I observed a person walking away from the area of that driveway. He was wearing a dark jacket and pants, which I believe were blue jeans. He also had on a red shirt under the jacket, and was carrying a box. It was a man whom I believe was a fellow by the name of Peters, whom Elaine Tyree objected to very strongly and had moved from 24 Columbus Street to break up her husband's association with Peters."

When Mrs. Tyree heard this, she immediately asked the man to write an affidavit so that she could use it in court. Mr. Gardner agreed and suggested she meet him at the office of his nephew, who was an attorney in town. This was because his nephew's secretary was a notary. This was the first time someone had actually placed Peters at the crime scene rather than in his barracks room on the day of the murder.

Bill recalls, "I was told off the record that there was an order from the SJC, dated July 6, 1979, which forbid the arrest of anyone in the murder of my wife. I knew that the crooked court system in the Commonwealth of

Massachusetts would never admit that such an order existed. Such a confession would be an admission that the murder of Elaine Tyree was truly a one-of-a-kind murder. So, I spoke to my mother. By this time in 1987 my father had died. So, explained the situation to my mother and away she·went. On her own, she filed for criminal charges against Earl Michael Peters and Chief William Adamson. In their zest to bend over backward and defend Peters, the Droney DA machine filed motions on behalf of Peters and, toward the end, they finally produced the order dated November 20, 1979 "

It is important to remember that Gaye Tyree was acting "pro se" during this time. On April 10, 1987, Magistrate Thomas Cotter, sitting by special appointment in the First District Court of Northern Middlesex County, denied the request for criminal charges to be brought against Earl Michael Peters and former Chief Adamson, without providing a written reason for this action.

Never being one to take "no" for an answer, much like her son, Bill, Mrs. Tyree filed for a rehearing on April 13, 1987. The requested criminal complaints were denied again after the hearing was closed to the public. Her subpoenas to bring forth four witnesses were denied, and the Middlesex district attorney openly defended Earl Michael Peters once again.

Erik Aarhus also wrote an affidavit in 1987, which is as follows:

"I, Erik Aarhus, do hereby attest to the following:

That I do not remember anything of my arrest.

That I have no memory of making any statement to the police or implicating myself in the death of Elaine Tyree.

That in and during 1978 – 1979, I was having serious problems with drugs (narcotics), up to and including my arrest. My immediate supervisors in the army at Fort Devens, Mass. knew about my drug problem, but refused to get me the help I needed. The reason I am told is that I wasn't late for work and that I could still perform my duties as supply clerk at the riggers section.

That what I have read of the alleged statement attributed to me about my alleged involvement in the death of Elaine Tyree doesn't match up with the physical evidence produced by the police. And that according to witnesses, I was at the Service Company mail room during the time that the crime was supposed to be happening.

That the alleged statement (confession) was coerced by Chief Adamson of the Ayer Police Department. I was not cognizant of making any statement, nor did I knowingly, freely, or voluntarily give any statement to the police."

Signed, Erik Aarhus

Another affidavit came forth from a fellow soldier and friend of Bill's named Ken Garcy. In his affidavit, he states:

"That I am and was aware that between January 1978 and January 1979, that Mr. Tyree was under an intense investigation by the Fort Devens CID.

During that investigation, I was specifically told by CID Agent Joseph Burzynski that the CID 'would get Tyree.' The reason, according to Burzynski, was that he refused to cooperate with CID in any fashion. It is rare but I have seen the CID proceed against other soldiers as strongly as they did against Mr. Tyree, but only when they were directed to do so. The CID wanted Mr. Tyree because their investigation was at a dead end with no leads and Mr. Tyree stood fast, refusing to cooperate with the CID.

During a routine CID interview, the CID offered me a number of deals if I would help them get Mr. Tyree. The CID also threatened to make my life miserable if I didn't help them get Mr. Tyree. I refused all offers by CID. Then CID went so far as to intimidate me by attempting to search my parents' home, which my mother refused to let them do."

Mr. Garcy's affidavit also speaks of a friend of his, a fellow soldier named John Newby, who died in a routine HALO parachute insertion training mission at Fort Drum, New York. Prior to Sergeant Newby leaving for Fort Drum, he told Garcy about Operation Orwell. He informed him that he should speak to Colonel Cutolo, who was commander of the 10th Special Forces Group (A). He told him that Colonel Cutolo was recruiting soldiers trained in communications. He also recalled running into Earl Michael Peters after Bill had been arrested. Garcy said that Peters appeared to be nervous and informed Garcy that he believed Bill to be innocent. Garcy even went further to relay another incident that shortly after Bill was arrested in 1979, he ran into insurance agent Ernest Maguire and a fellow soldier, Steven Wolski. During the conversation, Mr. Maguire informed the men that it was common knowledge that Ayer Police Chief William Adamson was buying military property, guns, and drugs through certain criminal elements in the community.

In a phone conversation Ken Garcy had with Erik Aarhus in 1993, Aarhus stated, "Naw, Bill wasn't down for what happened to his old lady. The only thing Bill did was turn me into the cops. Yeah, Bill had nothing to do with the murder. I said he did because he turned me into the cops. The cops said he turned me in. Then the cops wanted to know if insurance money was the reason Elaine was killed. So, I decided to get even and make Bill squirm a little."

Another matter arose after Bill Tyree was convicted; it was the matter of his discharge from the United States Army. After Colonel Rittgers left Fort Devens, he was replaced by Colonel Richard Kattar. When the discharge board met and reviewed Tyree's military record for discharge, Colonel Kattar wanted them to discharge him under circumstances other than honorable. His request was denied. The Department of the Army instructed Colonel Kattar to transfer Bill Tyree's military records. Eventually, Bill's records were transferred to Fort Dix, New Jersey, and he was discharged under honorable conditions in 1982. This was done as a direct result of someone at Fort Devens, possibly Lieutenant Colonel Lee Borden, a former Special Forces officer who knew that Bill had an exemplary record of service in Special Operations. Bill's DD 214 had been severely sanitized. The form only acknowledged that he was awarded the Army Service Medal. Meanwhile, his previous discharge form acknowledged a parachute badge and an M-16 marksmanship medal. It appears that Bill's personal 201 file had also been sterilized. Erik Aarhus was discharged and received a dishonorable discharge. The fact that Bill received an honorable discharge is extremely rare and unheard of since he was convicted of murder.

As a side note, Colonel Kattar was under investigation by Massachusetts Attorney General Francis Bellotti when he retired from the United States Army after serving as post commander at Fort Devens .Colonel Kattar was brought out of retirement and put on active duty for a couple months while the investigation took place. Bellotti discovered that Colonel Kattar had received a civilian job as payment for giving a sanitation contract to a certain company while post commander at Fort Devens. Eventually, the whole matter was dropped.

In the early 1990s, an affidavit by Colonel Cutolo surfaced. He had died in May 1980 in England in a single car accident. The authorities ruled it an accident due to his drinking and driving. Cutolo's family, as well as several of his West Point classmates, have always questioned the circumstances surrounding his death, but no foul play could ever be proven.

In the document, Cutolo admitted to the existence of Operation Watchtower. He stated, "In February of 1976, I commanded the second Watchtower Mission into Colombia. This mission was twenty-three days long and ended with only one reportable incident occurring between team members and a Colombian Army unit. There were no fatalities received by Watchtower team members. There was no indication that the Colombian Army unit sustained fatalities. The purpose of Operation Watchtower was to establish a series of three electronic beacon towers beginning outside of Bogota, Colombia and running northeast to the border of Panama. Once the Watchtower teams (Special Action Teams) were in place, the beacon was activated to emit a signal that aircraft could fix on and fly undetected from Bogota in Panama, then land at Albrook Air Station. The cargo flown from Colombia into Panama was cocaine."

He continued, "In 1978, I assumed command of the 10th Special Forces Group (A) at Fort Devens and recognized two soldiers. The two soldiers I recognized were assigned to the 10th Special Forces Group. One was assigned to Special Forces Operational Detachment Alpha in 3rd Battalion, Sgt. John Newby. The other had just been reassigned off an Operational Detachment Alpha following a criminal investigation division matter being levied against him. PFC William Tyree was reassigned to a Forward Support Team but had been carried for the preceding month on 2nd Battalion's roster."

The affidavit proceeds to go into great detail about the events of January 30, 1979. It continues, "On January 30, 1979, at approximately 1147 hours, two men were dropped in the parking area of the apartment complex where PVT Tyree resided. One man was identified as Erik Aarhus. The second man couldn't be identified due to his face being covered, as the two men entered the apartment building where the Tyree family resided. Surveillance indicated that at least one of the two men entered the Tyree apartment and left prior to the arrival of PVT Tyree and his wife at noon. Following a scream, local police were notified. The first police car responded quickly and a single officer entered the building. After the officer entered, one of the two men exited from a window on the ground floor of the building. This window was identified as the Tyree bedroom window. The man seen leaving this window was identified as SP4 Earl Michael Peters."

According to the affidavit, Colonel Cutolo had the Tyree apartment under surveillance and informed Bill of what he knew on January 31, 1979. It states that Bill informed Colonel Cutolo of the diaries and that they contained information on Watchtower and Orwell. The document then states, "Upon PVT Tyree leaving my office, I initiated contact with Massachusetts State Police lieutenant John Dwyer, of the Middlesex District Attorney's Office. Lt. Dwyer had cooperated previously on Operation Orwell and understood the urgency of the situation, and Lt. Dwyer notified me that during a search of the Tyree apartment, he discovered the diaries behind the refrigerator with a note to the family of Elaine Tyree. He did not disclose the contents of the note. Shortly before noon on February 2, 1979, I received a telephone call from Lt. Dwyer. He indicated he would drop off the diaries belonging to Elaine Tyree at my office. Upon receipt of the diaries, I reviewed them, noting much of Operation Watchtower and Orwell was written throughout the many pages of the diaries." The document continues with information concerning CIA matters and government money laundering.

The affidavit, however, was never signed, and the information contained within it is speculative at best. Even Colonel Forrest Rittgers Jr., who personally knew Colonel Cutolo and had a personal knowledge of the way Colonel Cutolo would phrase things in his reports, stated to me personally that he did not believe the document was written by Colonel Cutolo.

Around this time, Bill put in a request to the CID for all records under the Freedom of Information Act. Mixed among the documents he requested was a one-page CID investigation report form.

The form stated, "On 27 February, 1978, this agent interviewed PV2 Elaine A. Tyree HQ CO USAG, Fort Devens Mass 01433, as a possible candidate for the informer program. On 8 April '78, this agent was assigned as her handler. On 30 January '79, PV2 Elaine Tyree was the victim of a homicide. Homicide occurred at PFC Elaine Tyree's off post residence at 104 ½ Washington Street, Ayer, MA. 01433. Homicide occurred at approximately 12:04 p.m. Agent handler will assist civilian police, but at this stage will not disclose PFC Tyree as member of the informant program."

The rest of the document is blacked out and the bottom of the page is signed by CID agent Joseph Burzynski. Burzynski has denied the authenticity of the document, but does, however, acknowledge that it is his signature. CID agent Mason has tried to discredit the document although another independent retired CID agent has viewed the document and believes it to be authentic.

After the Cutolo affidavit surfaced, retired United States Army colonel William Wilson, an old friend of Colonel

Cutolo, felt compelled to investigate the alleged Latin America narcotics operation identified as Watchtower. Colonel Wilson teamed up with retired Chief Warrant Officer Mr. McCoy, who had been an MP, a CID investigator, and a private investigator upon his retirement from the army. They interviewed nearly two hundred witnesses regarding Watchtower and the murder of Elaine Tyree. Their five-year investigation yielded overwhelming evidence of Operation Orwell and Watchtower. They also found evidence of a conspiracy by parties unknown related to the murder of Elaine Tyree.

On September 4, 1998, Bill Tyree filed a lawsuit for $63,000,021 against the CIA, George Bush Sr., Scott Hershberger, and Paul Cellucci. The basis of the case was the refusal to return personal property such as photographs, uniforms, and personal diaries that were seized by the Ayer Police Department. The suit alleged that George Bush Sr., as director of the CIA and drug trafficking activities, ordered the theft and destruction of Elaine's diaries prior to her murder. The suit alleged that Bush and the CIA were part of an ongoing criminal conspiracy to bring drugs into the United States. The complaint that Tyree filed was 101 pages long and also contained supporting affidavits that were approximately five inches thick. Paul Cellucci, the former Republican governor of Massachusetts, was once the attorney general of Massachusetts. While at that post, he investigated the Ayer Police Department and discovered theft and corruption on a massive scale. Tyree made several appeals and motions, to which Cellucci failed to respond. Hershberger, who was the attorney general of Massachusetts at the time Bill filed this suit, was named for failing to comply with court orders to return Bill's personal property that allegedly would prove his innocence.

On April 29, 1999, six attorneys showed up in court to defend Attorney General Scott Hershberger and

Middlesex district attorney Tom Riley from the criminal complaint issued by Bill. Both men were being charged with receiving stolen property and non-compliance with a court order to return Bill's property. The judge ultimately dismissed Tyree's complaints on grounds of venue, but did not challenge or dispute the ten-year-old jury verdict or the order to return Bill's property. Allegedly, the attorneys representing Hershberger and Riley approached Bill's attorney and hinted that they may offer him a pardon. However, that offer never came.

One of the most interesting affidavits in this case came from a woman named Dee Ferdinand. The following is a portion of her testimony to attorney Raymond Kohlman:

Raymond Kohlman: Okay. Was there anything else about Sandman?

Dee Ferdinand: Just that there was an Operation Sandman. It was an assassination team for certain people that needed to be eliminated through the agency. He used to talk about a fellow by the name of Sandy, who was a Green Beret at the time, which he had been with him and worked with him.

RK: Had he worked with this Green Beret, Sandy, a lot?

DF: I think on numerous occasions he kind of liked him. He used to say that he was very good military material.

RK: Did he ever identify this Sandy by any other name?

DF: No. The only thing Dad used to say was first of all he knew him. His father was in the military. Dad had worked with his father in something to do with forklifts and mustard gas. Okay. He knew him through that and I think it was around the late 70s, Dad would discuss this kid, Sandy, and that he had gotten himself in trouble and they were trumped up charges because of what this kid knew.

RK: Did your father mention where these charges were made?

DF: In the New England area.

RK: Was he any more specific about New England?

DF: It was the Green Beret out of Massachusetts. The Fort Devens area. A colonel my father knew, Colonel Cutolo. It had something to do with Colonel Cutolo.

RK: So now your father mentioned Colonel Cutolo in relationship to Sandy the Green Beret supposedly out of Fort Devens, Massachusetts.

DF: Yes.

RK: Did he say Cutolo was in Massachusetts?

DF: Yes.

RK: Did he know Cutolo from Massachusetts?

DF: He knew him from the military. They had worked together and he had originally known Ed Cutolo, I think, from the Bronx area when they were kids. I think from the Bronx or somewhere in the New York area when they were kids.

RK: Above and beyond what your father said about Cutolo, are there any other indications that he knew Cutolo?

DF: Well, I had wound up finding Cutolo's daughter, JJ. She was living here in Albuquerque and I had found her because at this point, things were getting a case of the crazies of looking for people that Dad knew, trying to confirm, deny, and JJ had come to the house and she had seen a picture of my dad and she identified my father. She had met my father on occasion. She knew who my dad was.

RK: Did she say where she met him?

DF: Fort Devens and she had met him one time in Florida someplace.

RK: So, in effect you got the sense that Colonel Cutolo's daughter…

DF: Oh, definitely met my father. Definitely.

RK: Okay. Do you know if this Sandy, Green Beret from Massachusetts, is still alive?

DF: Yes, he is.

RK: He is alive?

DF: Yes, he is.

RK: And where does he reside?

DF: Walpole, South Walpole Prison.

RK: In what state?

DF: Massachusetts.

RK: How did you find out that Sandy was alive in Walpole, Massachusetts?

DF: I had been talking for a while to a gentleman by the name of Bill McCoy. Bill McCoy and I were having quite a few conversations and I kept on telling him that I had to find this guy, Sandy, who was framed for a murder because of what he knew as far as operations, Black Operations.

RK: Excuse me. Let me interrupt you. How do you know he was framed because of his knowledge of... Oh, well, first of all, let's define what do you understand Black Operations to mean?

DF: Illegal operations that are not sanctioned by the Congress.

RK: And where did you get this definition you are using?

DF: My dad.

RK: So, your father would, one way or another, say that if it is a Black Operation, Congress doesn't know about it?

DF: Exactly.

RK: Okay. So how did you get the impression that Sandy was framed because of his knowledge of Black Operations?

DF: I didn't get the impression, my father told me. When my father got really sick, he felt that he had to clear this kid's name.

RK: Okay. So, your father got sick in '85 and your father passed away in '90. During that five-year stretch, can you narrow down when he told you this?

DF: He stated in '85 that he had business that needed to be taken care of, that only he could take care of because it seems that there was some type of diaries that were in my father's possession at one time that my father had brought to CIA headquarters in Langley, Virginia.

RK: Did he say when he had these diaries? When they were in his possession?

DF: In the '70s.

RK: Did he indicate early '70s?

DF: No. It was the end of the '70s. Like '79, maybe going into '80. Maybe toward the end of '78, somewhere around there. It was the end of the '70s.

RK: Okay. So, let's get back to Mr. McCoy. You were having a conversation with Mr. McCoy?

DF: Quite a few conversations with Mr. McCoy.

RK: Okay. And how did Mr. McCoy lead you to Sandy?

DF: Okay. I was led, let's say Sandy was led to me. Sandy had called Bill McCoy to tell him that he needed to find JJ Cutolo and that she was in the Albuquerque area.

RK: Now, how did you know that?

DF: Bill McCoy told me. He called me and said to me, 'You're in Albuquerque, can you find JJ Cutolo?' And I said I will try. He had told me that she had worked for a radio station so I said okay. I will try to find JJ for you. It was ironic because I had been looking for any family members to do with Colonel Cutolo. I had asked Bill McCoy about speaking to Colonel Rowe's wife, Nick Rowe, and he told me that I couldn't because she was very afraid of what was going on since her husband's death and she refused to speak to anyone. To make a long story short, I picked up the phone and called information and found JJ Cutolo in Albuquerque and I told her that Bill McCoy needed to speak to her because a man by the name of Bill Tyree needed to speak to her. I asked Bill McCoy who is William Tyree and he said to me, he is a Green Beret who is charged with the murder of his wife, Elaine.

RK: Okay.

DF: Bill McCoy did not want to put me and Bill Tyree together.

RK: Did he say why?

DF: No, and Bill McCoy knew my father's whole story and it is odd because he would talk to Billy about Dee in Albuquerque but never mentioned Dee was Colonel Carone's daughter, so Billy was discussing things with Bill McCoy on Colonel Carone, but Bill McCoy never told him that he was talking to me.

RK: Is Mr. McCoy available to talk to?

DF: No, Bill McCoy is deceased. He died last year, October.

RK: October 1997?

DF: Yeah.

RK: So, basically through Mr. McCoy, you have identified who Sandy is?

DF: I had told Bill I would not give him the information on JJ Cutolo unless I was able to speak with Bill Tyree so that was the deal, and Bill Tyree wrote and asked me. In the meantime, Bill Tyree had gotten a newspaper called the *Free American* and there was the story of my dad in the *Free American* and my name was in there. Billy called Bill McCoy and they had been discussing Colonel Carone, but McCoy never told him that Dee and Desiree Ferdinand in Albuquerque were the same, so Billy wrote me a letter. Billy identified himself and then he asked me in this letter if I would possibly know him by his, I guess you would say code name or call name, or whatever, and the name was Sandy, which I did not believe at the time because my father used to say the kid's name was Sandy because of his light-colored hair. And when I saw a picture of Bill Tyree it was a newspaper clipping and what I saw was black hair in this newspaper clipping until I spoke to his mother and asked her.

Dee Ferdinand's father was Albert Carone, a New York City Police officer, with ties to the five organized crime families in New York City. He had also been a colonel in the army. Shortly before he died, he became disillusioned with the way the United States government had been doing business under the guise of national security. This was when he began informing his daughter, Dee, of what his real job had been for so many years: he had acted as a bagman between the CIA and organized crime. According to her, the CIA would bring drugs into the country and the Mafia would distribute them, thereby funneling the money back to the CIA for its Black Operations. Her deposition further stated:

RK: Now, these diaries he had mentioned that he had, did he mention who they belong to?

DF: Sandy's wife.

RK: Did he mention any names?

DF: Sandy's wife, she had diaries.

RK: Was he more specific about that?

DF: The diaries could harm a lot of people in the military.

RK: Did he say how?

DF: Only that they can do harm to a lot of people within the military.

RK: Was he any more specific about identifying the diaries?

DF: In what sense?

RK: Color?

DF: Blue.

RK: He stated that they were blue?

DF: They were in his possession.

RK: Right. Did you see them or did he tell you they were blue?

DF: I saw the diaries.

RK: How do you know they were the diaries?

DF: He said that they were Sandy's diaries.

RK: So, your father.

DF: Sandy's wife's diaries. Let me straighten that out.

RK: Right. So, your father identified them as Mrs. Tyree's diaries?

DF: Sandy's wife's diaries.

RK: So, he only identified them as Sandy's wife's?

DF: Yes.

RK: Okay. How many were there?

DF: I do not remember. I cannot tell you. There were a couple of them, I know that. And they were not the type of diary that kids have, you know, that they have the lock on them or anything. They almost looked like a thin telephone book, memo type.

RK: Did you at any time that your father had them get an opportunity to look at them?

DF: No.

RK: So, all you knew was that there were some diaries, they were blue, and they were identified as Sandy's wife's and that they were dangerous to military people. Did he mention any particular military people?

DF: No.

RK: Did he mention any location of the military people?

DF: No.

Then she told a rather amazing story:

RK: Did Mr. Tatum indicate to you that he knew your father?

DF: Yes, he did. He said that he was the pilot that brought my father from, I think it is Camp Drum in New York, to South America on a couple of different occasions and he also stated to me that he knew at one time he was witness to the fact of George Bush being with my father in South America.

RK: Did he indicate what time he saw George Bush and your father together?

DF: No, he did not. I think he told me they were in the Honduras region. My father was passing himself off as George Bush's private doctor.

RK: Did you have any indication of anything else about Mr. Bush?

DF: I don't understand your question. They were running drugs.

RK: Mr. Bush?

DF: Yes.

RK: With the assistance of?

DF: Mr. North and quite a few others.

RK: Have you ever been able to identify Mr. Bush?

DF: Ex-president of the United States, George Bush.

RK: How do you know it was George Bush?

DF: Because my father said at one time he was. Number one, the president of the United States is involved, and if all of this information came down it would bring down the Oval Office. Number two, he was involved with drug running because my father worked with him when he was with the CIA.

These allegations were just the proof that Bill Tyree needed to help substantiate his claims of Watchtower and that Elaine kept diaries on certain activities for which she was killed. Unfortunately, the court dismissed the case and downplayed the evidence Bill and Dee attempted to introduce. What the Court did not realize was that Bill had proven the existence of the diaries and the fact that they were sent to the CIA to assist in covering up the larger conspiracy of shipping drugs, specifically cocaine, into this country for over forty years.

Bill has reconnected with his former post commander, Colonel Forrest Rittgers Jr. They, along with friends Ken Garcy and Hank Aamsden, have currently been working on another attempt to get Bill the fair shake he has been denied since 1979. For nearly forty -two years, Colonel Rittgers was under the impression that justice had been served for both Bill and Erik Aarhus. It was not until recently that his view of those events changed. After reviewing the probable cause and trial transcripts, he has come to the conclusion that Tyree and Aarhus were denied justice. He has since filed an affidavit and recanted his authorization to search the barracks room of Erik Aarhus. The conclusion of this latest legal maneuver is yet to be seen.

"Well for one, the Thirteenth Amendment to the Constitution of the US, which abolished slavery, did not abolish slavery for those convicted of a crime." Angela Davis

CHAPTER NINE

Surviving Incarceration

Bill's life today is much different than it was in early 1979. He states, "This was my first encounter with the law. The first and last. I was sentenced to life in prison for Elaine's murder. Most of my friends are still in the military and they always ask the same question: 'If you had to sum it up in fifty words or less, what's it like in there?' There is no silence. There is always noise somewhere. There is no privacy. There is always someone watching you. There is no darkness. There is always a light on somewhere. Dostoyevsky said that the degree of civilization in a society can be judged by entering its prisons. Well, if Dostoyevsky was to enter the prisons in Massachusetts, he would be in for one hell of a surprise.

"In 1980, when I was introduced to the joy of doing time, the prison system was on its final days. The Feds were everywhere. A lot of their clones were running the prisons. The clones were taken to federal prisons and taught the orderly operation of corrections. Why ? Because you can't have a police state using private prison contractors like (Jackson) Stephens, Inc., unless the prison is controlled. Private prison contractor Stephens, Wackenhut, Sandia, and even Bechtel all have plans for American prison labor. Why move their businesses out of America to a banana republic when they have those republics inside every single prison in America? Another fact of life in prison is that only the strong survive. You have to be strong physically or mentally. If not, you won't last.

"The headlines read, 'WALPOLE NEEDS A BILL OF RIGHTS, Fair and Humane Treatment for Prisoners, Safety for Guard.' Michael A. McLaughlin spoke to a Guards Union meeting on November 20, 1978: '... You have asked me to limit the subject of violence; so, I shall get right to the point. The single most serious threat to the safe operation at Walpole is drugs.' In 1978, there were five murders and eleven assaults on inmates by other inmates that warranted mention by McLaughlin. I read the so-called last word on Walpole, a book called *In Constant Fear*, and found the book lacking in many areas. Whether the pastrami caused a riot, the prison went into deadlock, or the longest prison lockdown in the history of America or the longest prison lockdown in the history of American corrections. It was all part of a plan to bring the Massachusetts Department of Correction (DOC), into line with the bigger picture.

"In order to use prison labor to make money for Wall Street, you would have to reduce or provide better treatment for AIDS infected inmates, curtail or terminate media access to the prisons. That is not so easy when it is already acknowledged that many inmates are isolated due to their beliefs. One way to ensure total control over the prison with the total support of the prison would be to suggest that the nine prisoners were ripe recruits for a terrorism cell. Regardless of whether you like it or not, the prison system is your doing. It is a reflection of what your system is.

"Currently in the Massachusetts DOC, back-to-back judicial decisions that have been litigated to a conclusion, which began in 1993, have found that a lack of adequate programs inside a prison translates into a ten times higher chance of the man going back to prison. That means the Wall Street weenies get more of your tax dollars while the man incarcerated is held for $38,000 to $40,000 per year. Think about that racket. Here are a few more thoughts about prison that you probably don't know and have never thought about:

"Medical: currently $3.00 per visit to the Hospital Support Unit (HSU);

"Employment: for most inmates, the normal pay is $1.50 per day;

"Notary services: $1.00 per page;

"Phone: collect calls only. $4.94 for the first minute and $.65 for each minute thereafter. The calls last thirty minutes, then you have to pay the first minute fee all over again;

"Visits: normally contact. At MCIW (Massachusetts Correctional Institute Walpole) all non-legal visits are non-contact, through a glass with a phone. Normally two visits per week. One hour in duration;

"Food: three meals each day. Normally overcooked or undercooked. Then there is the chow hall. You have to know someone to get a chair. Or in the alternative, you have to take someone else's chair; that has medical issues attached to it, brings $3.00 for the HSU.

"Haircuts: $1.50. Styles available, none. If you don't like the haircut, make sure you have $3.00 for the HSU.

"Sports: weightlifting, street hockey (yes, with sticks). Baseball, softball, and football were banned at MCIW. Why? A lot of people were showing up in HSU and they didn't have $3.00.

"Canteen: no cans, no can openers, no lighters, no cigarettes, no clippers. They do have black and white televisions $122.06 (retail outside the prison for $45.00 to $55.00); color 13" for $245.04 (retail outside the prison $75.00 to $85.00); plastic typewriters $136.50; typewriter tapes $4.94 to $8.24 per pack of one tape! Whatever you get, it will be mashed or busted open and leaking in some respect. Why? Because you get the groceries in clear plastic trash bags that you have to give back to the guard.

"Disciplinary: from my personal favorites. I received a disciplinary report, (DR) for pouring cleaning solvent into the toilet in the staff bathroom. My crime? An officer said I was urinating in their toilet even though the stall was wide open and I emerged from the stall with the bottle of cleaning solvent in my hand and not my manhood! The inmates who mailed a bomb out of the prison over twenty years ago; the inmate that would call his native Puerto Rico on a phone he had hidden inside his GE super radio. He ran the wire to a wall outlet he had found. He also used it to monitor the guards in the main inner control room; the inmates that punched out another inmate, then drug his body over the band saw used in the kitchen to cut up the meat. The only problem is that the plug to the band saw was out of the reach of the inmate attempting to slice and dice the other inmate, so no cutting occurred! Or the inmate that hid in the back of the priest's car and escaped; or the time the wall actually caved into the exercise yard at the old MCI-Concord, in Concord, Massachusetts.

"Dental: currently the dental operation at MCIW is not worthy of comment. Confessions are available by appointment. You take your life into your own hands. My personal favorite, the night I had four wisdom teeth pulled and the gums were not stitched up. I bled through my pillow and was too weak to get up the next day.

"Best riot experience: as I lay face down with my hands cuffed behind my back, ankles shackled together, wearing a pair of underwear, I saw a K-9 dog bite an officer in the ass. The dog and the officer had prior issues and the dog had a long memory. If that had been an inmate, it would have been a $3.00 experience!

"You get used to the cage you live in; the people that never shower or brush their teeth; never change the two uniforms they're given to wear; comb their hair; never stop screaming, laughing, or complaining. The DOC commissioner described the ingenuity of an inmate in the following manner. He said, 'If there were three phone poles, fifty feet apart, and on top of each pole was one inmate, and I gave one inmate a match, one inmate rolling papers, and the last inmate tobacco. When I came back one hour later all three inmates would be smoking, and they would never have climbed down from the pole! I think that is how I would also describe the general populations I have been in.

"I have traveled all over the world. I had to come to prison to understand the human condition. To see men stand up for other men. Until you have witnessed men stand up against 12-gauge shotguns with nothing but their bare hands, you have not lived. Until you have seen these men take down another man they didn't like, you don't understand strategy. Until you have been in an exercise yard that is suddenly under fire from the guard towers, you really don't understand confusion and vulnerability. Until you have been set upon by a Move Team of guards dressed in motorcycle helmets and padded uniforms, you don't understand resistance. Until you have been stripped naked and left in a cell with broken-out windows in the middle of January, you don't understand cold. Until you have seen a guard pour urine into your drink served with your meal, you don't understand revenge or patience. I have seen inmates wait for years to get even. But when they do, it's something to see. You boil hot water and melt plastic into it. Then scald your enemy and while he is yelling for help, you begin to break him down. First his knees. Then his elbows. Every single shot is perfectly aimed because your victim is in the world of pain no one wants to visit.

"Prison: it's where the sheer fact that you're there means you're not to be believed! You have no credibility. At every single DR board hearing you go to, the guard is believed over you. Every time you get into court, you have to bring the pope to make your case. Your family and friends visit but soon have a better reason not to come at all. I have seen guys start a sentence and a month later, they are on their own. I'm getting ready to start my forty-third year of incarceration. My family is still with me and many of my friends are still here. I am fortunate. Many of the guys inside the wall have no family or friends other than what they have in here. That breeds a closeness that is rarely seen in society. Prison is a place that society has no time for and which the politicians use to get elected. They are the forgotten and the expendable. That's prison.

"Prisons serve in many ways: slave labor; targets of public outcry and political motivation; line items on fat state government budgets; identification of citizens who allegedly act outside the law; and depopulation. By keeping men incarcerated, they are not able to reproduce offspring. You are able to eventually kill the seed of that family altogether. Is there a reason that the prison population is higher than any other country on earth? Do the math and remember that inmates are not counted as human beings.

"Prior to the murder of Elaine, I wanted to defend my country against the enemies that would destroy her. I can trace the roots of my family backward in the United States Army to 1847. My father retired from the army in 1969. I am the middle child of five children. My oldest brother served during the Vietnam War. My younger sister served with the 4th Infantry Division as well, both in the army. I have an older brother and sister, and a younger brother and sister. I have never been accused of bad mouthing my country. I do not bad mouth my country now. Rather, I bad mouth those that would destroy my country, the Constitution, and either kill, discredit by incarceration, or bankrupt anyone who opposes them. This is my story."

Whether you believe Bill Tyree is innocent of his wife's murder or that he hired fellow soldier Erik Aarhus to do the deed, several facts cannot be ignored. First of these is Bill's allegations about Operation Watchtower. They were confirmed in Colonel Wilson's affidavit, Dee Ferdinand's deposition, and through Secretary of State John Kerry's efforts. John Kerry did document in a 1988 Senate report (The Subcommittee on Terrorism, Narcotics, and International Operations of the Committee on Foreign Relations of the United States) that the CIA traffics drugs. The Kerry Report, as it came to be known, detailed that personnel assets from the CIA trans-shipped cocaine into the sleepy town of Mena, Arkansas. Yet no criminal prosecution occurred at the state or federal level. The reason for the lack of no criminal prosecution taking place was due to national security. Whether Secretary of State Kerry knew about Operation Watchtower or Operation Orwell in 1979 when he was an assistant district attorney securing the secret grand jury indictment against Bill, we can only speculate.

There were several questionable acts by the Ayer Police Department and the Massachusetts State Police. They claimed they had fingerprinted the apartment but never released those findings in court. They did not do an adequate job of securing the crime scene, especially when Mr. Gardner was allowed to pick up the bedroom window screen and attempt to place it in his vehicle before being stopped by Ayer Police officer Walter Decott. Nor when Police Chief Adamson was warned about witness tampering by Judge Killam. Both law enforcement agencies failed to secure a search warrant for the crime scene, thereby allowing them to never have to inventory anything they removed from the premises, such as the alleged diaries.

The United States Army CID investigators, Burzynski and Mason, should never have been allowed to participate in the murder investigation of Elaine Tyree, due to the possibility that they were biased and prejudiced against Bill because of the Article 15 investigation. Also, it has been alleged through documentation that Burzynski was Elaine's handler when she was a CID informant. Another interesting point is, why would Bill have trusted Aarhus to kill his wife since he had already lied against Bill during the Article 15? Then there is the question as to why, after the murder, Bill was placed under guard and Dennis Testagrossa and Earl Michael Peters were selected for this job. Peters and Tyree were both under suspicion for theft of military property. Another soldier should have been selected for this duty. There is Colonel Cutolo's failure to initiate an Article 32 hearing. Finally, there is the CID agents' failure to wait until Aarhus had sobered up before taking his statement, along with the multitude of other failures ranging from chain of custody issues in the search to the lack of protocol in all areas of the investigation.

When the probable cause hearing took place, why was the Commonwealth of Massachusetts so hellbent on getting a conviction on Bill that they backed up the hearing with a secret grand jury indictment? Were they hedging their bets? There is the matter of Ayer Police chief Adamson coaching witness testimony; why was he not prosecuted for his misconduct? Then there is the bugging of the Ayer courthouse and eventual destruction of the evidence tapes, preventing Bill from proving his case that his rights were violated.

When the trial came, Erik Aarhus refused to testify against Bill. This gave Bill no way to cross-examine Aarhus or his redacted confession in any way. Vias Williams, the soldier who lived across the parking lot from Bill and Elaine, had informed the police that he witnessed a person running away from the Tyree apartment on the day of the murder. He is insistent to this day that it was not Aarhus, yet he was never called to testify in the probable cause hearing. However, he was called to testify at the trial, but the notice was sent to his former Ayer address. No one ever thought to ask the army where he had been transferred to.

EPILOGUE

Exoneration: The Long Wait

In the course of this book, I have touched on specific problems plaguing the cases of Bill Tyree and Erik Aarhus. It is easy to look at these two criminal cases and pick apart not only the blatant errors, army incompetence, and outright disregard of these two men's constitutional rights. I can also expose the flaws of the American jury system, a system that has been attacked over the years on a number of grounds; among them the claim that juries make mistakes in believing the wrong witnesses, drawing the wrong inferences from circumstantial evidence and, in worst case scenarios, sending the wrong people to life in prison or to succumb to the death penalty.

There is virtually no remedy to fix a factual error by a jury. There is no record of a jury's deliberations, and jurors are generally considered legally incompetent to testify as to why a certain result was reached or even how each juror voted as the deliberations went along. Of all the errors, cover ups, and incompetence that these cases have, the overriding fault is the fact that the wheels of justice grind on, and innocence becomes progressively less relevant. A man may be innocent of a crime, but once a jury convicts and the proceedings of the court are correct, the man no longer goes to any court in the United States of America to suggest that he is innocent. The mere suggestion would be irrelevant to the court, whether it be an appellate or a reviewing court.

The frustration of the entire process comes from the small space of a trial in which innocence can be established. This is where the hypocrisy of the criminal justice system truly lies, the promise of a fair trial.

If a man receives a fair trial, he still may be convicted and sentenced to life in prison—or worse, death—even if he didn't do what he was convicted of. Justice Felix Frankfurter said, "Due process is not a yardstick. It is a delicate process of adjustment inescapably involving the exercise of judgment by those whom the Constitution entrusted with the unfolding of the process." It serves that purpose well, but does not do much for factual accuracy. The judicial system is screwed up from the indictment process on. When a grand jury is convened, the prosecutor looks at the members as a flock of sheep and leads them toward the finding he wants. Tyree was arrested and indicted by a grand jury simply because either no other suspect could be found or was allowed to be arrested by the Massachusetts SJC.

It is also important to remember that when a defendant pleads not guilty, this is another way of saying "prove it." In Bill Tyree's trial, the Massachusetts Court's hideous little scheme worked like a charm. They successfully transferred the burden of proof to the defendant.

It has taken me years to realize it, but even if Tyree and Aarhus get out of prison, they will forever be condemned men. They cannot get their lives back. All the years of strain and tension have taken their toll. Even if they were to be pardoned or have their convictions overturned, a large portion of the population will always consider them guilty. Sadly, William Tyree and Erik Aarhus are still serving their sentence. Tyree has never relented in his claims of innocence. Unfortunately, if the Massachusetts court system ever discovers that they didn't commit the crimes they are accused of, there are some within the ranks who would strongly oppose ever letting this injustice become public.

There will always be a group of people who will argue and defend the American justice system and law enforcement. They will refuse to believe or even entertain the possibility that corruption and self-serving interests could be motives that factor into the criminal prosecution of an innocent man. To this group I can only say that the Ayer Police not only were inepter than the Keystone Cops not only in this case, but in the Kenny Waters case as well. They did everything but throw pies at each other. In an unrelated case, the FBI in Boston entered into a devil's deal with organized crime boss, James Whitey Bulger. In this case the FBI allowed Bulger to run his criminal empire for over twenty years unopposed in South Boston. FBI agent John Connolly was Bulger's handler in the FBI confidential informant program. He assisted the FBI in bringing down the Boston faction of the Italian Mafia by informing on them. All the while, he continued to participate in criminal activity such as drugs, extortion, and murder. He was able to avoid state and local prosecution during this time because he was being protected by the FBI. So, it is not that far of a stretch to consider the possibility that if an FBI agent could break the law, US Army CID agents could do the same thing.

The biggest red flag of this entire case is the location of the alleged murder weapon. How stupid does the CID or a third party think a jury, an investigator, or anyone else, for that matter, could be to believe that someone would hide a suspected murder weapon under a pillow? Even a child could do a better job of hiding an item. Yet the CID, the Ayer Police, and the Massachusetts State Police, all seasoned and highly trained investigators, never even thought or questioned the ease of the room search. There was no DNA testing in 1979. Law enforcement only tested the knife discovered in the search to compare the blood type of the blood found on the knife to Elaine's blood. Most criminal cases have no DNA evidence to test. Tyree has requested the Massachusetts courts test the DNA on the knife. The court has so far refused.

All the evidence that has been presented in this book does not prove Bill Tyree's or Erik Aarhus's claims of innocence. The evidence does, however, raise certain critical questions such as, are the Massachusetts courts and federal, state, and local law enforcement agencies guilty of complicity in the framing of two innocent men? Other questions that arise are: is this a malicious prosecution, false imprisonment, perjurious testimony, suborning perjury, and a complete violation of civil rights? Law enforcement conduct cannot be discretionary in any area of police work, because it clearly violates the Constitution. All these questions and the evidence does prove that Tyree and Aarhus have been denied their rights to due process, which has resulted in these men's imprisonment. It is also particularly revealing that in the many thousands of pages of pretrial testimony, no one, especially the defense attorneys, appears to raise the question of the Massachusetts Supreme Judicial Court's protection of Earl Michael Peters.

We all know the awesome power the government has over our lives. It becomes even more evident when it is trying to take away a person's freedom. We live in America, the land of the free and the home of the brave. We believe in fairness, equality, and especially, justice. When we discover a pattern of concealment and arrogance in the very institutions we have placed public trust in, it weakens our Constitution and our nation. This miscarriage of justice has had a profound impact on several people's lives and has caused immense human suffering not only to these men and their families, but to the victim's family as well. The lesson to be taken away from this case is that transparency and accountability must be present in every criminal investigation and prosecution. Everything in secret degenerates, even in our justice system. The failure of any man to be afforded a fair trial should enrage every American, especially since our Constitution promises it to everyone. If the efforts of the CID, State, and local law enforcement were to protect a guilty man and prosecute and keep innocent men incarcerated, then this would be one of the greatest failures in the history of the American judicial system, the State of Massachusetts, and the US Army.

PHOTOS

Verbeck Gate which is the main gate at Fort Devens.

Headquarters building at Fort Devens.

Colonel Shakavilli on the left and Colonel Cutolo on the right at the change of command ceremony for 10th SFG (A) at Fort Devens.

Riggers shed at Moore Army Airfield. This where Erik Aarhus worked. The woods behind the building are the alleged location of where the murder weapon was stored and hidden for two weeks after the murder.

The apartment building at 104 ½ Washington Street in Ayer, Massachusetts. The Tyree apartment was in the lower left corner of the building.

Army photo of Elaine Tyree

Army photo of William Tyree

This building was the headquarters for 10th SFG (A) for 2nd and 3r battalions on Fort Devens.

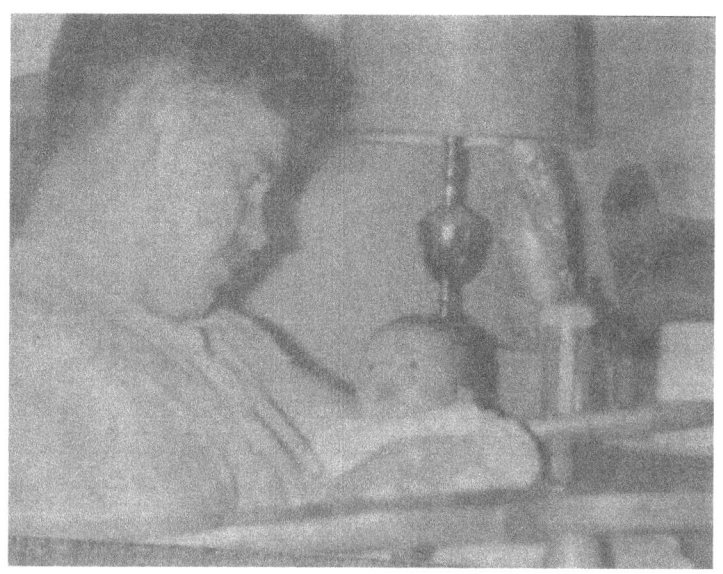

Bill Tyree and daughter Dawn taken at the Washington street apartment during happier times.

Change of Command ceremony for 10th SFG (A) at Fort Devens. Colonel Rittgers is the man with his back to the camera holding the guion. At the time he was the post commander of Fort Devens.

Author photo William J. Craig

AUTHOR'S NOTE

I have met Bill Tyree in person. He does not come across as a liar or someone with something to hide. Rather, he is man with something to prove, entirely consumed with proving he is innocent of the crime for which he has been convicted. He is very typical of any Special Forces soldier you may meet. He is fiercely independent, highly intelligent, and undoubtedly courageous, which some might perceive at times as arrogance. Very typical of an A-type personality. I have trained with Special Forces soldiers during my time in the army and what many might perceive as a social or personality disorder is instilled in them during training. They are America's frontline guerillas, trained to think independently and adapt to any situation in order to overcome any and all obstacles to complete their assigned mission. With that said, I must also state that Bill Tyree is tougher than any person I have ever met. He has had his life stripped away from him for over forty years. An event such as this usually brings most men to their knees, and yet he rises every morning with a quiet strength and continues to fight the good fight. He truly embodies the quote by Sir Winston Churchill: "Never give up. Never surrender."

Let me begin by saying this book has been in the making for over eleven years. In 2010, I began this project by contacting William Tyree and proposing that I would like to delve into his case and write a book about it. I impressed upon him in my letter that I would like his assistance in obtaining his version of this case. However, I let it be known that I was not going to write a story that would paint him in a glorified light. I informed him that I would be presenting the facts of the case through eyewitness accounts, court transcripts, and documents. I also told him that I would remain neutral and only insert my opinions if I found flaws in the case or legal procedure in order to bring them to the reader's attention. He wholeheartedly agreed to my terms and thus began my journey.

All accounts and quotes were obtained either in personal interviews, by telephone, or directly from sworn statements that came directly from court transcripts.

It has been a monumental undertaking accumulating and sorting through not only the mountainous volumes of paperwork, but also tracking down witnesses who are still alive. After this task was completed, I then had to separate the facts from the vast mountain of falsities and fiction that has grown around this case over the years. The end result is this book.

I want to further address the elephant in the room with this case: the conspiracy theories involving Operation Watchtower. These theories constantly surrounding this case are just that. It is important to remember however that America's Special Forces, which were formed in 1952, can trace their lineage back to the operating teams of the Office of Strategic Services (OSS), which itself was a predecessor to the Central Intelligence Agency (CIA) in World War II. The OSS's mandate was much broader than that of today's CIA. In addition to espionage, they also carried out paramilitary operations that seemed to go hand in hand. It has been proven that the CIA has been involved in everything from attempts to overthrow unfriendly governments to spying and importing narcotics. There are those who believe that Elaine Tyree's murder was orchestrated by one or more of the mechanisms of the Deep State. While it is true that there are many unanswered and troubling questions concerning those who were involved in Watchtower, including the death of Colonel Edward Cutolo, this book deals in facts, not speculation. I have touched on these subjects but only as they relate to the case.

Over the course of the last ten years, I have also had the pleasure of getting to know Tyree's inner sanctum, most commonly referred to as "the Elves": Ken Garcy, Colonel Forrest Rittgers Jr. (retired), and (General) Hank Aamsden, whose rank of general is an honorary field grade rank that was given to him by retired US Army Colonel Rittgers as an inside joke for his years of selfless service to Bill Tyree and his fight for freedom. It holds no military title or significance except with the above-mentioned individuals.

Ken Garcy has been able to help us understand the mindset and culture that surrounded the enlisted force at this time in history at Fort Devens. He has been instrumental in giving a very detailed and extremely accurate psychological analysis of the individuals whom he personally knew who were involved in the events of 1978-1979.

Colonel Rittgers Jr. came into this case approximately forty years after he testified at the probable cause hearing. I contacted him one evening by phone for an interview. As we discussed the long-ago events and evidence that has come out over the years, he began to have some questions. I had him get in touch with Hank Aamsden to discuss his concerns further. As they talked and the months passed, the colonel read every bit of documentation on the case that he could get his hands on, even reviewing his own personal files. He eventually came to the conclusion that Tyree and Aarhus were not given a fair shake by the Massachusetts judicial system and has since become another lone voice in the wilderness seeking justice for these two men.

Hank Aamsden has been involved with this case and been a personal aide to Bill Tyree for over twenty years. He has been there for him as a friend, confidant, and even a whipping boy when Bill becomes frustrated with his case and his fate since 1979. Hank has driven us all crazy over the years with his cryptic style of writing in his emails, which may be why a private is never allowed to write an after-action report in the army. Hank is a God-fearing man who has spent the last twenty plus years attempting to shed light on this case, with hopes that the Massachusetts judicial system will undergo a conversion similar to that of Saul of Tarsus, who became Paul the Apostle on the road to Damascus.

Yet these men and myself all have a common bond. We have all served in the US Army and refuse to leave our fallen brothers behind. Guilt or innocence is not for us to say. We have a duty to make sure that our government and judicial system abides by the Constitution of the United States, which we all have sworn an oath to defend, and that oath didn't come with an expiration date. These individuals have shown much kindness to a total stranger and have welcomed me into the fold. They have been of great assistance with this book and have helped to raise legal issues and insightful questions that may have been overlooked without their help and for that and their friendship, I am eternally grateful.

A special mention needs to be made to the following:

Retired Concord Police detective Paul McGrath for his first-hand knowledge of the Ayer Police Department and Massachusetts State Police who worked in and around Ayer during the time of the late 1970s and early 1980s. He was instrumental in helping me understand the mindset and culture of the time.

Retired CID agent Carl Craig, who was instrumental in reviewing the CID agents' actions and exposing failures to follow standard CID procedure at the time and giving me a crash course in CID criminal investigative procedures. Mr. Craig served twenty-two years in the CID before retiring. He then went to work for the South Carolina State Police and served an additional twenty-two years before retiring as a detective lieutenant. After retiring from the State Police, he started the Cold Case Homicide Unit for the Richland County Sheriff's Office, where he served without pay for twenty years before his passing in 2017. His knowledge and insights in regards to this case helped make this book possible.

Honorable James W. Killam III, who spent many hours with me dissecting every move he made during the probable cause hearing that ultimately led to his controversial decision. Unfortunately, this wonderful man passed away before the completion of this book, but his contributions will forever be remembered.

JJ Cutolo, daughter of Colonel Cutolo, for sharing her memories of her father and his service to our great nation.

If I have left anyone out it wasn't intentional, for many have contributed in multiple ways and to all I owe a debt of gratitude and a heartfelt thank you.

DEDICATION

To my children, Meadow and Danica, always remember: "You cannot choose your battlefield, God does that for you; But you can plant a standard where a standard never flew." *The Colors*

For More News About William Craig,
Signup For Our Newsletter:

http://wbp.bz/newsletter

Word-of-mouth is critical to an author's long-term success. If you appreciated this book please leave a review on the Amazon sales page:

http://wbp.bz/watchtowera

www.ingramcontent.com/pod-product-compliance
Lightning Source LLC
Chambersburg PA
CBHW061140120626
46546CB00005B/1872